Seventy Businesses You Can Start

With A Few Hundred Dollars - *OR LESS*!

Plus advice on how to launch your business and build your sales

by

Robb Roy Taylor

Most of the businesses can be run from home by a man or woman on a part-time basis, or full-time if unemployed. Many are unique with no competitors.
Most do not require special skills or abilities

ISBN: 1-4140-6644-9 (e-book)
ISBN: 1-4140-6645-7 (Paperback)

Library of Congress Control Number: 2004090574

This book is printed on acid free paper.

Printed in the United States of America
Bloomington, IN

1st Books - rev. 03/09/04

TABLE OF CONTENTS

ABOUT THE AUTHOR

Robb Roy Taylor was a NYC Marketing Consultant to major corporations before re-locating in 1962 to Fort Lauderdale, Florida where he began selling businesses. He sold motels, sightseeing ships, cocktail lounges, restaurants, and all types of small businesses. In 1966, with a merger-acquisitions boom going on, he went back to NYC and opened an office on Madison Avenue. Within a few months he was selling companies and arranging mergers.

In 1981 he put together two giant corporations for what was then the biggest merger in U.S. business history. He took his six-figures commission and returned to Florida, living in a high-rise pent-house with a 32-foot Chris-Craft cruiser docked below and in other ways enjoying a life of sun, sand, and surf.

This idyllic life-style came to an abrupt end in October 1987 when the stock market nose-dived, wiping out most of his assets. It was back to selling businesses.

Robb Roy retired from business brokerage in 1999, but today, concerned about the high rate of unemployment and a need by many families for additional income just to maintain their life-style, he wrote this book. It reflects 40 years of experience. Robb Roy believes each of the businesses can produce a good income if one is willing and able to put in the necessary time and effort. Most can be started on a part-time basis, from home, if presently employed, to see if the selected business produces income and satisfaction.

Each can be launched for a few hundred dollars -or less!

DISCLAIMER

This book is presented by the author and publisher for the purposes of describing various types of businesses which may be of interest to those thinking about starting a business on a part-time basis working from home. It is not intended as a complete guide to the success of any of the businesses described.

The author and publisher shall have neither responsibility nor liability to any person or entity for any losses or damages caused directly or indirectly by the information in this book. Many of the businesses described are highly- creative ideas not yet proven to be money-makers. There- fore this book should be used as a source of ideas rather than as a handbook on operating a small business. For that latter purpose are hundreds of books on managing a small business. Be warned: every business represents a gamble -and the odds depend upon who is running it. But don't focus on the negative aspects of owning a business. With that focus nobody would own a dog.

PREFACE

So you would like to own your own business? Or maybe you just need to make some more money while you hold onto your present job? Just as most people want to own their own home rather than renting, many individuals who now are employees want to own a business rather than *renting* their time and talents to an employer.

But only a small percentage of wage-earners will take the big step of quitting or resigning their job in order to start or buy a businesses. After all, it's a big gamble! If you have fixed expenses to pay --a mortgage, car payments, a hefty credit card debt, tuition, alimony and child support payments, or other fixed expenses, that gamble can be very risky.

Okay, to get to work you may have to drive in heavy traffic, or ride in crowded, public transit? And you may be living by the clock -getting up at a fixed time to be at the job at a fixed time no matter what the weather or how you are feeling, going to lunch and back at a fixed time, working until a fixed time - . Hey, if you aren't in control of your time that could qualify you as a "wage slave." Today, many enlightened employers recognize that rigid control of employees' time is counter-productive and, like time-clocks, becoming obsolete.

Or maybe you must put up with the authority of a boss you don't like or with fellow-employees you don't like and in both cases must pretend otherwise? Or, maybe you believe that your real potential will never be achieved in your present job or with present employer. either because of office or work politics or limited opportunities for advancement? One of the worst situations these days is not knowing whether you are going to be laid-off or not, for reasons beyond your control? The uncertainty can be nerve-wracking. It's not surprising if you are thinking about having your own business - even just as a precaution against a possible reduction in work force.

Easing Your Way Into A Business

Most wage-earners cannot afford to buy a business or go without a pay-check for very long. Today, with rising prices for almost everything, most employees usually need more money just to maintain their accustomed life-style despite a regular paycheck. (The government keeps telling us there is no inflation. Yeah!   Right! How about chicken parts selling for over $3.50 a pound at the supermarkets, and rents and home prices soaring?)

One solution to a money problem is to start a part-time business that can be run from home without giving up one's job. Hopefully, this book will contain a business opportunity that appeals to you and which will become so successful you eventually can quit your job and run it full-time. I hope so!

Disadvantages of Owning A Business

1. In most cases you will work harder than for an employer -- and with longer hours, at least for the first year.

2. In most cases you won't have any net income (take-home money) for several months, will have to live on your savings.

3. You will have to fight the tendency to put things off while you enjoy your new- found freedom and leisure.

4. You will have to make decisions in areas where you have no experience or skills (such as bookkeeping, purchasing, pricing, sales promotion, etc.).

5. You will experience much tension as you risk the capital you slowly acquired over the years and wrestle with doubts about the decisions you are making.

6. You will feel all alone and miss the companionship and help of fellow-workers.

Advantages of Owning A Business

1. You set your own hours; no longer have to live by the clock, fight commuter traffic, or squeeze onto crowded transit

2. You no longer have to please the boss(es) or put up with annoying co-workers or nasty customers.

3. You will have more time for family matters, your spouse, your kids, your friends, for hobbies, recreation, your community.

4. You will have more prestige among your peers and in your community.

5. You will not have to abide by a dress-code. With a home-based business you can work in your pajamas.

6. No ceiling on your income. Your abilities and drive will determine how much you make.

7. You can live in any geographic location you choose.

8. You can control how much taxes you will pay.

9. You will be doing work you enjoy.

10. You interact with other business owners

Note: If you want to buy a going business rather than start one, this is the wrong book to read. See best book on How To Buy A Business in the "Books" section. We sell all recommended books **below publisher's list price!**

BUSINESSES TO AVOID

MLM (multi-level marketing) This is a business that depends upon your getting recruits, those recruits getting more recruits who, in turn, also get recruits until many levels of people are in your "down line." The system almost always breaks down   Most MLM schemes (that's what they are) involve sending out mailings. The usual return is one or two percent. Suppose you send out 1000 letters at 37 cents for a postage cost of $370. Then there's the cost of the envelope, the copy- machine letter and any insert, which we'll say all totals ten cents. That adds $100 for a new total of $470. Then you need a mailing list of 1000 gummed labels that will cost at least $75. Your out-of-pocket costs now are $545 and you have put in many hours of folding, inserting, sealing, affixing labels, etc. Say you get a one percent return (ten responses). Each response has cost you $54.50. But you need to make a profit, so what you are selling must be priced at $75 or more. How many people are going to send you or your "down line" $75 or $100? - especially if you print your sales message on a copy machine using colored 20 lb.

paper with glaring, black headlines and misspelled words, as most MLMers do?

Most MLM solicitations promise earnings of $3000 to $5000 a month and up and cite case histories of "ordinary housewives" and high-school drop-outs, now rich, standing alongside a luxury car in front of a palm-studded mansion. Think for a minute! If you actually could make $3000 to $5000 a month from mailing out a few hundred letters would not the promoters hire minimum wage workers for about $250 a week to do nothing but send out mailings? And if someone is a millionaire why are they trying to get a measly $25 to $100 from you instead of enjoying their "wealth?" As for the MLM schemes that involve gifting (sending money as part of a chain letter), fogedaboutit! Those who claim to be making big money from these chain letters are lying.

Restaurants

You picture yourself as a genial, smiling host greeting people who just love the food your restaurant serves. But probably about one in ten restaurants survive the first year --and that one is because the owner is working his butt off sixteen hours a day, has no home life, is able to put up with lazy, low-grade help and the prima donna chefs (who are the most important element in the business), and the constant complaining by finicky customers whose food is too hot, too cold, too spicy, not spicy enough, too well-done, too rare, etc., etc. Owning a restaurant is one of the toughest businesses you can get into.

Vending Machines

Sounds great! You just go around once a week or so to re-stock the machines and collect thousands of dollars from the bulging coin boxes. But the most important element in this business is getting locations -- and good locations are difficult to find. The ones supplied by the vending machine seller usually are bummers (competitors will pay thousands of dollars for a good location) and those supplied may cancel out after a few months (to be re-sold to the next investor). If vending machines actually produced thousands of dollars a month in profits the makers wouldn't sell them to you. They would own the machines themselves, hire minimum wage workers to restock the machines and empty the coin boxes.

Franchises

Almost all franchise offerings are intended to enrich the franchisors, not you. You are asked to pay an exorbitant franchise fee (like $35,000 for a gift store franchise) then pay a royalty **off the top**, that is, before you pay for expenses, rent, salaries, etc. You could end up paying thousands of dollars a year to the franchisor even though you are losing money. *There is hardly one franchise that could not be operated with greater success using your own business name -- and that goes for hamburgers and pizzas. Everything depends upon how well the business is run, on the quality of the product (wouldn't you prefer a burger made with freshly-ground, round steak a half inch thick, to the long-dead, frozen and thawed meat that you get at burger chains?)* Perhaps ten percent of all franchise offerings are even worth the initial fee and the royalty on sales. Again, if the franchise really could make the profits claimed, the franchisors would run their own stores using $300 a week managers. Name value? - 80 percent of franchises have none that matters to shoppers.

Flea market Operations

Some people do okay with a table or booth in a Flea Market. but mostly these produce little income. It is a business for a certain type of person -- one not bored to death by just sitting around most of the day making an occasional sale for a few dollars profit. If you are handicapped a Flea Market business may be just the thing for you, but there are so many easier other ways to make money, as you will find when going through this book. However, many Flea Market exhibitors enjoy the socializing that goes on among the other Flea Market sellers.   Be cautious about renting space in an *indoor* Flea Market. Your income will depend upon how much money the owner(s) will spend to stimulate traffic. After an initial advertising blast, many owners spend very little because you are obliged to pay a monthly rent under the lease, (unless it specifies that a certain percentage of rent income will be spent on stimulating traffic- rare!).

These are just a few of the businesses you should be wary about starting. However, if you still believe a franchise is the way to go, look for a book on that subject in our "Books" section. We sell books at below list price.

LOCATION OF YOUR BUSINESS

"Location" is NOT important to almost any business in this book. Most of the businesses can be run out of your house or garage, a rented storage space, or a tiny office in a low rent area. If working from home or garage you may want to check with the zoning office in your town or county to find out whether it is permissible (however, most people running a business from home wait until the neighbors or the officials give them a hard time, then get needed permit or license).

It sometimes is a good idea to have a rented space, so you will get out of the house to go to work. Otherwise you could spend most of the morning lounging around, watching TV or playing with the kids, and finding other excuses not to get to work. Self-discipline is an important factor in making a business successful. And if you are out of the house you won't get bugged by your spouse to do things around the house, like fixing that leaking drain pipe or making sure there are clean shirts or the kids' favorite brand of cereal.

Some businesses can be operated out of a truck or station wagon or SUV, or even the trunk or rear seat of your vehicle. In any case, it is important to keep costs low. Be wary about signing a long-term lease in your enthusiasm and about buying office machines or special tools until you are really socking away big dough. For example, if selling pre-owned gowns or other clothing a suitable rack can be made from low- cost, white PVC pipes bought at local home-improvement store.

In short, it is advisable to conserve as much cash as you can and to avoid commitments involving a steady outflow of cash. Look into renting what you need until rental costs equal or exceed the installment payments required when purchasing.

IMPORTANT NOTICE

You can start many businesses by renting the equipment you need. Visit a Rental Equipment store and find out what items they rent and which are rented most often by people running their own business. You may get ideas for a business you like?

In this book are more than a dozen businesses in which rented equipment can be used to reduce the costs of starting up. One example is a moving business. You can use the various advertising and promotion ideas set forth in this book to let people know you handle moving jobs --big or small. You should group the jobs on the same day. You then can rent the right size truck for $29 a day or so. You are in the moving business. See more details in this book under the heading "Moving Business."

You also can rent all the furniture needed for an office. including desks, chairs, copier, computer, etc. Once you have proven that your business venture is a good one, you can think about buying the things you need for long term use.

A great many examples of using rented equipment to launch a business can be given, from airplanes to tractors, but you get the idea -- let the business produce the capital needed to pay rental costs, whether it is equipment, a storage space, or an office. If renting an office or workshop or warehouse try to get it on a month-to-month basis. The essential idea is to conserve cash.

That said, let's look at the 70 businesses described in this book

70 BUSINESSES THAT CAN BE LAUNCHED
FOR A FEW HUNDRED DOLLARS - OR LESS!

ASTROLOGY CHARTIST

This is going to be seen as an "off the wall" business to many readers, but, hey, mapping people's astrology chart can be a very profitable business run right from your dining room table and so, deserves consideration. It is a good business for a woman because, for some reason, it seems like a feminine activity. Yet, a large number of males are involved in astrology charting.

Now, astrology is seen by many intellectuals as a pseudo-science, but about 40 percent of Americans say they believe in the forecasts of astrology and use them to make important decisions. Almost every newspaper runs an Astrology column. Are newspapers stupid?

Do you remember that Nancy Reagan, when First Lady, used the services of an astrologer to provide advice to the president of the United States? Listen, many corporations are paying hefty fees to astrologers for help in strategic planning and the selection of candidates for top-level jobs.

How do you run this business? You get information from the client on date, time, and place of birth then use a standard chart to calculate the sun sign, moon sign, and the location of the planets at the time of birth. Each sun sign has a known personality profile.

(Described at length in Linda Goodman's paperback "Sun Signs"). Next, you calculate the forces operating on that profile as of the present time and what those forces may result in?

If you are new to astrology you will need to study up on the techniques involved. When you are able to develop an accurate chart, it is worth $50 to $250 and more. Today, there is computer software to help make the chart. Is this a legitimate business? You betcha! Astrology has been around for thousands of years. Not one geneticist has been able to determine the effects of planetary electromagnetic waves on the new DNA configuration in the fertilized egg cell (zygote).

This can be a very profitable and interesting business. Don't go into it if you think astrology is just a primitive superstition. You'll fail. What's *your* sun sign? Why do you know it? (*See Index for Book and reference sources*)

TGIF PARTIES

If you live in a town or city of over 15,000 population you can make an arrangement with a well-located cocktail lounge to hold a "Thank Goodness -It's Friday" party for business people. It could be held every Friday from 4.30 P.M. to 6:30 P.M. You could have a circular printed announcing the parties and emphasizing it is a good place to meet people of both sexes and to perhaps make good contacts for doing business or getting a better job offer. The circular should be distributed to all the offices and retail stores you can reach, possibly with the help of a couple of high school students. You also could run small ad in biz newspaper, but should try for free publicity (Ask Chamber of Commerce, Rotary Club, etc. for support, send details to local newspaper.).

Make arrangement with the cocktail lounge for a fixed, slightly lower than usual, price for drinks and ask for (say) 25 cents commission per *mixed* drink served. The lounge should supply things like popcorn, potato chips, pretzels, etc. (Point out to lounge owners or managers that many partygoers will stay afterwards for drinks and perhaps dinner).

You make money mostly by charging a small admission fee (say) $3 or $4. Tables and chairs are not needed for everyone (have only a few)-- most of those attending will want to stand and to circulate. If everyone is at a table the party will be deadly dull. Discourage sitting at the bar ('It's for regular customers, not for the party-goers").

Ask everyone to put their business card in a container for a prize drawing in final hour (Could be an imaginative $10 item). If you live in a city of over 30,000 population you run several parties at one time *in widely separated locations*. There could be very low background music just to create a "party-atmosphere." LOUD music is a no-no. It will interfere with the chatting that takes place and chatting is most important to attendees. Again, it is a big mistake to have tables and chairs. The partygoers should stand and circulate.

Let's suppose 60 men and women attend first party. That's $180 to $240 for you. Then suppose they order a total of 100 drinks. With a commission for you of 25 cents that's another $25. So, running one of these parties could give you $200 gross, every

Friday! If you run things so people enjoy the parties, attendance could shoot up to over 100. Do the arithmetic! There's money to be made on a part time basis.

With this party experience you may wish to run singles parties on a Wednesday or Saturday nite. Could be a fun biz.

TALENT MANAGEMENT

Attend places where they have karaoke and "Talent Nights." When any of the performers display exceptionally good talent (singing, dancing, comedy, musical group or instrumentalist), approach them, give them your business card ($10 per 1000 at Staples) and ask them to contact you by phone. You card should give your name with "Talent Management" underneath. When they call, explain that you are impressed by their talent, that you are putting together a small, entertainment group that will put on weekend performances locally at condominium complexes, social clubs, perhaps at nite clubs. They will get paid something, but the objective is to give them professional experience and groom them for a show-biz career.

An important person you will need to sign-up is a good keyboard player for back-up music. You then will have to find "gigs" (bookings) for your group of entertainers.

Another thing you can do is find musicians to form a trio (keyboard or piano player, guitarist, drummer) and then book them into local nightclubs to play for dancing. You may be able to book more than one trio, collect up to 35 percent of the pay, depending upon how high a price you negotiate.

Some States require a talent management license (easy to get). When you find that any of your entertainers have great audience-appeal, offer them a 1-3 year contract during which you will seek to obtain TV and nite club appearances (send out a photograph and an audio or videotape to local TV stations and to top nite clubs, including those in Vegas, Reno, NYC, L.A., etc.). If your client goes over big the contract could be sold for big bucks to a top-flight, talent management company. Meanwhile, holding the contract could give you 10 percent or more of earnings.

This is a business for a person with a winning personality, able to act out the part of a professional manager. It has the potential for big earnings -- eventually! It is NOT a short-range money-maker, but ideal if you can do it while still employed. *(See "Recommended Book" on this subject)*

SPEAKERS BUREAU

Organizations, clubs, businesses, trade associations, and other groups continually use speakers to enliven a program or to train or inspire others. They can turn to you for help in locating right speaker for their audience and their purpose.

You will have little difficulty signing up local celebrities (elected officials, chiefs of police, chefs of upscale restaurants, newspaper editors, major builders, physicians), and other prominent, local people. Most of these will deliver a speech without charge, but some will want a small honorarium, such as a luncheon or dinner, being picked up and returned by taxi, and perhaps a few dollars or a small gift. Your fee for booking the "right" speaker for an occasion could be $75 to $150.

In some cases, the group will want a well-known celebrity as a speaker. You should compile a list of prominent Speaker Bureaus and their clients (easy to obtain) and the fee wanted for the celebrity you are interested in booking. You then can make an arrangement for a commission on the fee to be paid because the booking will be handled locally by your office. You will have to arrange to meet the speaker at the airport or train station (some celebs won't fly), and arrange for hotel accommodations if there is an overnight stay, plus get the speaker back to the airport. A member of sponsoring group often will want to accompany you. Payment is in advance.

When working with another Speaker Bureau your cut should be at least 15 percent of fee being paid to speaker. Don't hesitate to go for big names on the national scene--such as Congressmen, authors, show biz celebrities, etc.You need not limit your activity to home town -- try to reach groups in entire area using small display ads, direct mail, etc. This is a business that can be run from home in spare time with small investment in stationery, biz cards, mailings, and perhaps a few lunches or dinners with top man or woman of groups which call on you to obtain speakers.

NOTES ON THIS BUSINESS:

TAKE "FAKE" SNAPSHOTS OF CELEBRITIES

Here's a fun business for an outgoing person. It requires just a couple hundred dollars investment and, yet, can produce $100-up per day,up. Using a good Polaroid camera and a tripod you take snapshots on the street of people standing next to life-size, cardboard cut-outs of famous people --like Bush, Clinton, Elvis, movie stars, sports figures, etc. You put the snapshot into a cardboard frame readily obtained for about ten cents each. Anyone looking at the framed-photo might think the pose with the celebrity is based upon a real meeting.

You can charge $5 to $10 per snapshot (depending upon economic conditions in your area). You will need to set up on a busy corner. You also could take the snapshots indoors at tourist locations, at gambling locations, at country fairs -- any place where a large number of people congregate (such as rock concerts, holiday celebrations, etc. etc.) Where do you get the cut-outs of celebrities? (They cost $25 to $40 each) -- do a computer search of "Celebrity Cut-Outs." Some sources are: Elifesize, (800) 216-9728; Advanced Graphics, San Francisco

21

(800) 488-4144; Ahl.com; Valudisplay.com (888) 421-4241; austinstar.com; celebritystandups. com --- and several others. Ask for free catalog of available, life-size cut-outs. The president cut-outs are popular. You could start by doing this on week-ends. It's a fun business, a money-maker.

You may be able to rent a top-grade Polaroid camera before investing in one of your own. Buy film in quantity at discount. Practice your photography, using friends, before charging for photos. The paid-for photographs have to look real.

CONSIGNMENT ART DEALER

If you have an interest in art here's a business that can be very satisfying, as well as lucrative.

Using your credit card if necessary, buy from a wholesale art house several pieces of framed art which you believe will have broad, general appeal, perhaps a mixture of traditional and modern pieces. Your cost range should be $30 to $80 because you want to re-sell these pieces for at least three times your cost. You also could attend local art exhibits and get some local artists to let you sell their paintings on a commission basis through your consignment-selling program.

You then call on upscale restaurants and get them to let you hang three or four pieces on their walls, ideally where people wait to be seated and where there is enough light. You will have to learn how to hang pictures so they are secure. A framing store can show you how.

The pieces of art can add a classy, upscale ambiance to the restaurant. *It is important that frames be impressive and expensive-looking!*

Each piece should have a classy, easily-read corner card (reverse side of your biz card?) which gives retail price. The restaurant can be given a commission of (say) $20 per piece sold.

Each restaurant may sell one or two pieces per week. If you eventually have (say) ten restaurants selling your framed art, you could earn $600 a week and more.

You can do the same thing in nearby towns when you have the money to buy many pieces at a time (By buying from one wholesaler you may be able to establish a line of credit whereby you pay for the art in 30 to 60 days). You soon will get a real feel for what kind of art sells in each restaurant and the retail price range most popular (usually $95 to $195).

You should list the pieces of art loaned to each restaurant and get a signed receipt from them which shows the retail price. What is nice about doing business through restaurants is that they are able to accept credit card payment from buyers.

You may be able to find other outlets for consigned art, such as gift stores, upscale furniture stores, etc. *Warning! - before you buy the pieces of art, tour the*

*upscale restaurants to find out whether someone
has beaten you to it in your area.*

NOTES:

CONSIGNMENT JEWELRY

A great place to sell low-price jewelry is in beauty salons. Patrons there will buy items on impulse from a small rack set up on or near the counter. The rack, available from several suppliers, could consist of only two or three shelves and two rods on which can be displayed earnings, bracelets, charms, necklaces, rings, and costume jewelry pieces.

Each piece should carry a small price tag, so employees will not be interrupted with "How much does this cost?"

Your first task will be to locate a suitable supply of nice pieces of costume jewelry on which you can make *at least* twice your cost. Look up wholesale jewelry suppliers in a library directory. There are a great many of them. The most important step is to visit salons and get them to let you put in your rack in exchange for a commission of (say) one fourth of the selling price. (You should be able to show the type of jewelry you will be offering and their prices). Salons should be glad to put in a rack! -- they can earn over $200 per week, over $800 a month from the rack - enough to pay their rent!

When you have racks in many salons in your town or city and perhaps neighboring towns, you will take in a nice income.

Have the salon owner or manager sign a receipt for all the pieces of jewelry and the rack, then visit each salon once a week or every two weeks to collect your money and restock the racks. Before committing yourself to this business, visit salons in your area to find out whether they already are selling jewelry and whether they are willing to participate. Some may even decide to sell their own jewelry. Point out that continual buying, restocking, and maintaining the rack and paying bills will interfere with their main business. You also could put racks in upscale, women's clothing boutiques.

NOTES ON THIS BUSINESS:

OFFER A SEMINAR

If you have special knowledge of a subject (or can acquire it through reading), you can offer a seminar on that subject. If you are not a self-assured, good public speaker it is easy to find one to work on an hourly basis (perhaps $25 an hour?).

The topic must have wide appeal to either the general public or to business people or to workers involved with that subject. Rent space for $100 or less to accommodate (say) 50 people (usually at a hotel, but could be YMCA, a church or club meeting hall, etc.) The seminar should be no more than two hours, say from 7:30 to 9:30 in the evening or, for business people (company paying) 4 P.M. to 6 P.M on a Friday.

You will have to advertise the seminar at a cost to you of perhaps $200 and use other promotional methods (see section in this manual " **Sales *Promotions")**.* If you attract (say) 30 people at $29 each you will take in $870 for a take-home profit of $300 to $400. Run the seminar twice a week.(Tuesdays and Thursdays are best)

You can earn $1000 a week or more if you attract 40 or 50 people at the appealing low price of $29. (Some seminar professionals charge $150 or more for business seminars). After the first few seminars you could switch location to other nearby cities. In fact, you could run a seminar every evening from Monday to Friday, enjoy having the daytimes for recreation, family matters, etc.

(See best book on this subject in the "Recommended Books section)

MOBILE DOG GROOMING

Grooming a dog usually requires the owner to bring the animal to a pet grooming parlor and wait for it -- which could be a nuisance for busy people. Since everything needed to groom a dog can be carried in a case, it makes sense to offer a grooming service done in the home of dog owner. One woman who offers this service had 300 repeat customers after only one year.

Don't know how to groom a dog? It is not difficult and a license can be obtained in most States without having to take a training course or pass a test. To get experience offer to groom the dog of friends or neighbors without charge -- if they will stand by and watch and give suggestions. You also could volunteer to take their dog to a grooming parlor, going to the ones where you can sit and watch the proceedings -- and find out about prices being charged for various grooming services. You also can find books in the public library that deal with this subject.

In addition to doing the grooming (or hiring people to do it on a commission basis) you also can sell pet products, (flea collars and preparations, leashes, fragrances, etc.) and perhaps a unique line of dog food (not locally available) to be delivered every two weeks or so. Don't enter this business if you are afraid of dogs or dislike them.

For ideas on how to build this business see the "Sale Promotions" section in this book.

NOTES ON THIS BUSINESS:

HIRING HOUSEWIVES

Many stay-at-home housewives previously held office jobs and so, have telephone and clerical skills. When children are at school their mothers often have several hours in which to earn money. A large percentage of them want to. This is a big, untapped labor pool.

Find a product or service you want to sell and pay housewives a commission on each sale (not as employee). You can locate these women with a classified ad under the "Part Time Jobs" heading or by posting a notice on bulletin boards.

These women also can make telephone surveys for your clients, do computer typing, or make appointments for companies selling roofing and siding, air conditioning, hurricane shutters, etc. etc. If you can locate women who own a computer and are fairly skilled on it you could make a lot of money selling "outsourcing" computer services to companies.

You act as the "job getter," organizer, and supervisor If the women are to sell something they should have a "script" that gives them the words to say and which enables them to handle typical objections or "stalls" by prospects.

You could contact large business firms in your area to find out whether they want to "outsource" (farm out) computer tasks and occasionally need extra help to handle unexpected heavy (clerical) work loads. Outsourcing by companies is becoming quite common.

In short, housewives constitute an unused labor pool. Your task will be to find part-time work opportunities for these women.

When you have a large number of housewives working for you on a part-time basis your own income can be substantial.

SELLING USED BICYCLES

Buy them for $10 to $25 from classified ads and from police/sheriff's auctions of unclaimed, stolen items.

Do minor repairs (new tires if needed and new handlebar grips), lubricating the chain and other moving parts. Then do general clean-up, such as removing rust and restoring original paint (as with automobiles).

Once bikes are in good mechanical condition, sell them from your garage or from rented storage space. Kids' bikes are good sellers. Some stores selling new bicycles will pay you to assemble them. Contact them. You can often buy new bikes in "clearance sales" for little money. However, keep in mind that chain stores often will advertise new bikes for as little at $49. They are your competition. Run a small classified ad on continuous (contract) basis, such as *Used bikes, $25 up. Men's, ladies', kid's. All put in top shape. 000-0000.*

This business can be run a part-time basis -- doing repair work in evenings, making sales on a Saturday. You also could sell new wire baskets and other new accessories, such as wide seats for older folks and the tubbies. Additionally, you could make arrangements to sell very expensive bikes from a catalog. Some bicycles sell for several hundreds of dollars and cannot be bought at Wal-Mart or other such discount stores.

There are several "Bicycling" magazines that contain ads for the very expensive bicycles. Contact the mfr's to get an Agency for your area. They will refer your inquiry to a distributor. Don't overlook used, three-wheelers, They are ideal for senior citizens to get around with and can be very profitable to sell. To get started takes only a few hundred dollars, much of that in promoting sales to get started.

HOME REPAIRS CENTER

Become a central, contact source for those people needing home repairs or improvements. You should be able to refer plumbers, painters, carpenters, roofers --other providers of services to home owners. Most providers of services to home owners want more customers and will pay you a commission (say 10 percent) for such referrals. Have an Agreement in writing signed by suppliers before you make referrals.

Get feedback from home owners as to their satisfaction with quality, courtesy, pricing. Replace those suppliers who leave the home owner unhappy, but be sure to have a replacement.

You will need to run a small ad in newspaper and use other promotional tools in order to get calls from homeowners looking for help with "fix-up" problems. A separate phone line is advisable, with ringer turned off during sleep hours, or use an answering machine.

Some home repair companies you refer (air conditioning, plumbing, others) will offer an annual contract to the people you refer. Make sure you get a commission on such sales because the annual contract results in your losing a customer.

Your important task will be to become known as a central source for prompt, home repair and maintenance services by reliable local firms who charge a reasonable price and stand by the quality of their work with guaranteed satisfaction.

It may take several months before you are well-established but within a year you should be earning a good income from this business. It easily can be run from home. Its success will depend upon your ability to handle human contacts well.

ASSISTANCE FOR THE AGED

Assemble a group of housewives who are able to spend a few hours helping the aged by offering companionship, doing light clean-up, accompanying on errands, preparing a meal, etc. Charge of $15 per hour is obtainable in most areas, with the helper getting (say) $10 per hour and you getting (say) $5 for advertising, for getting the jobs, and for administration costs. Helper housewives should sign "Independent Contractor Agreement" (See sample in Index).

You have to find trustworthy Helpers and usually will offer their help only to aged women unless the male is an invalid or another woman is present (wife or relative). You may have to have the Helpers "bonded" (covered by an insurance policy in case of possible stealing or undue influence on financial affairs of an aged client).

You can get clients by using a continuing (contract basis) classified ad, by contacting Agencies that work with the aged, and also letting churches know about your services. Churches often have aged parishioners who can use help with daily chores and who can afford to pay for it. If an aged person cannot afford your help but needs it, look into State and federal government assistance programs for the aged poor. They may pay for your services to qualified recipients.

This is a business ideal for those who have compassion for others and want to do something helpful and satisfying. It can, however, provide a decent income for those who need more money to maintain their own life-style.

INSTALLING LOW-COST INTRUDER ALARMS

Many home-supply stores, such as Home Depot, Lowe's, and others, sell a low price intruder alarm for $100 to $150. The system consists of sensors which are attached to doors and windows. The sensors will send a radio signal to a small central console (placed in the bedroom or living room) that will sound a loud alarm if a protected door or window is opened even slightly.. This is the most efficient type of intruder alarm because what you want to do is scare away the intruder, not catch him in your house. You can earn $35 to $50 an hour for installing these simple systems. To get started. notify all sellers of such intruder alarms that you are willing to install them (takes about an hour when you are experienced. The door/window sensors have self-stick, adhesive backing).

You also can buy these systems yourself direct from the manufacturer for about $65 to $95 (cost depends upon how many doors and windows to protect) and sell them directly to home and condo owners and renters (system easily moved to another location because there is no wiring). Many people who have wired intruder alarms are paying $25 to $35 a month to have their system monitored by a telephone-answering service often located hundreds of miles away. Upon receiving an alarm signal the monitoring service will phone the homeowner. If homeowner does not answer, the monitoring service will call the local police. By the time police arrive it could be a half hour after intruder has gone with the loot. And, because so many of these monitored alarm systems deliver false alarms, the police now charge up to $150 per false alarm, many triggered accidentally by motion detectors in home.

In short, you can get into the security business for a few hundred dollars or just install these simple yet effective alarms in your spare time for $35 to $50 an hour for people who buy them at Home Depot or other stores and need help installing them. No electrical skill is needed. On-premise audio alarms are the most effective and economical way to have intrusion protection.

HOUSE-TO-HOUSE SELLING BUSINESS

If you live in an area with high unemployment it will not be difficult with a classified, "Help Wanted" ad to find men and women to do house-to-house selling PROVIDED you give them a good product or service to sell that will produce **at least** $50-$75 a day in commissions. They should be hired as Independent Contractors (See sample Independent Contractor Agreement in Index)

Women are best at this type selling because of gaining easier entry to the house. What can be sold? - indoor air purifiers, humidifiers or dehumidifiers, drinking water filtration devices, fire extinguishers, security alarms, exercise equipment or programs, computers, other major-purchase items that can yield a commission of _at least_ $20 per sale to the salesperson. (Don't try to compete with Avon Products, Tupperware, or other long-established giants). Some people have started this direct-selling type of business and now earn over $200,000 a year. Decide on the right product, then look up supply sources with a computer or in a public library Directory of Mfrs.

You will need to have an arrangement with a supplier who does not require you to maintain a large inventory, but who will make prompt shipments to you as needed. Don't hesitate to ask for 60-90 days credit on the products you buy from the manufacturer or distributor or supplier. They need business, too. Also, ask them for sales training aids -- booklets, films, tapes, etc. which you can use at Monday morning "pep" talks.

You also may want to consider the "Party"-type of direct selling, whereby a customer invites friends, acquaintance, neighbors, co-workers, etc. to a house party at which the salesperson can put on a demonstration. The "hostess" of the party usually is given free merchandise. The salesperson usually pays for the refreshments. Be on the look-out for personable women or men for your team who can keep the party-goers interested and/or laughing. Other party-givers are recruited at the party. Don't try to sell high-priced vacuum cleaners - now too competitive (Wal-Mart. K-Mart. Sears, Target, etc.). This business can grow into a big-time operation.

CONSTRUCTION SITE CLEAN-UP

Many home builders are glad to pay outsiders for cleaning up their construction site and taking the debris to the dump. Why? - because skilled construction help is hard to find and get a high hourly rate. Besides, builders have a schedule to meet. Two people generally are needed for site clean-up because there may be some heavy lifting.

Call on all construction sites. talk to foreman, quote an hourly rate of $20 to $30 (check rate with competitors) Don't overlook commercial building sites. You will need a truck. Rent one as needed. Otherwise, no investment money needed. You could hire people to do the work while you get the jobs and collect the money. That's the way fortunes are made. But if you don't have management and selling skills and are willing to do physical work, you can make good money cleaning up construction sites yourself with a friend. Also look for other types of clean-up jobs, such as at remodeling sites.

With all the home-building and commercial construction taking place these days, a site clean-up business easily can produce an income of over $600 per week - depending on your location. *(See related book in Recommended books" section).*

SUPPLYING PART-TIME LABOR

In areas of high unemployment many men and women are glad to get a few hours of minimum wage work every now and then doing non-skilled labor-- such as helping to move furniture, unloading trucks, painting fences, assistant to skilled workers. You can be the intermediary who supplies such labor, tacking on an additional two or three dollars per hour for your management ability. Get jobs by having a circular printed offering unskilled, part-time "as needed" labor. Distribute the circulars to all moving companies, factories, retail stores that make deliveries, condo and housing developments, hospitals, office buildings, etc. But first you will need to run a "Part-Time" Help Wanted classified ad, and meet those replying in your garage-office or at a convenient fast-food restaurant (buy them a sandwich and a drink if they are good candidates - not those smelling of alcohol). Have a pad of Employment Applications with you to get personal details. But don't look only for high-class types. Some of the jobs will be dirty work with no contact with the public. What you must look for is "dependability"--

individuals who will show up when needed and are willing workers - not shirkers.

You can specialize in providing "muscle" labor or even provide clerical help or people with specialized abilities, such as computer operators. Go in the direction you feel most comfortable with. One thing to consider -- you must be able to take early morning calls (like 7 A.M) from those needing workers. And must be able to reach your workers in early morning hours. All workers should be signed up as "Independent contractors." (*See sample Agreement in back*). Look into any State or local requirements for licenses.

Notes on this business:

BOOKKEEPING SERVICE (YOU don't have to do it).)

Every business needs to keep financial records, prepare statements and invoices, and other records, such as Inventory Control. Which businesses are usually lax about these necessary office chores? - - small retailers and one-person businesses!.

Distribute a circular to retail stores and small offices, particularly doctors and dentists. Can't do this kind of bookkeeping and accounting yourself? - run a classified ad under "Part Time Help Wanted" to locate housewives who previously did this kind of work but now have to stay home with the kids. Even if you can do this type of work yourself, it's a good idea to keep locating customers and thus expand your activities by hiring part-time, bookkeeping help, as needed.

Bookkeeping and accounting services can be built into a high profit business. The demand for bookkeeping help is growing because of local, State, and federal government bureaucracies demanding more data. They want tax money. But, even more important, businesses need data to determine profit and loss status and to adjust selling prices, etc. Because most people hate working with numbers your bookkeeping and accounting services will be in increasing demand, even if you personally can't add up a column of numbers. (See recommended book) .

AUTO & TRUCK WHOLESALING

You will need a wholesaler's license from the Department of Motor Vehicles. But it is easy to get and not expensive. And you will need a computer. Then, work from home or rent or share a small office. Run a 3 or 4 line classified ad in the "Automobiles For Sale" column on a steady (contract) basis. Your ad could say "Buy Your Car or Truck at Wholesale --Save Thousands of $." When you get phone calls find out what make and model is wanted, get details such as color preferences, acceptable mileage, price range. Then use the computer to find such vehicles at dealerships within 50 miles radius. When you locate a likely car, call the dealer, give your wholesale license number, ask for $200 commission on lowest price dealer will take. Then ask to take the car for a couple of hours (leaving your own vehicle) You soon will build a relationship with dealers.

You also can scan automobile classified ads in your area's newspapers and auto/truck magazines. In short, you are getting paid to search out a good vehicle for your customers. There are many other aspects to this type of business. For example, with a

Wholesaler license you can attend vehicle auctions, bring along a prospective buyer who will pay you at least $200 over the auction price of the vehicle wanted.

This is a satisfying business for someone who likes and knows something about vehicles. It can be run from home, preferably with a two line telephone, so personal calls are separated (necessary if you have a teen-ager at home).

Notes on this business:

NEWSLETTER PUBLISHING

This is a business that can produce a good income for spare-time effort. It helps if you are a competent writer, but if you are not, write as well as you can and then get someone to edit the copy. One doesn't have to be a maker of literature to turn out a newsletter. But ya shud be literit. The newsletter should look professional. Get design help if you are not good at designing. Pick up design ideas from other newsletters.

The most important element is *a good topic!* What do you know that other people will pay to find out? If you don't have anything of importance to convey to a specific group of readers, pick out a subject you are interested in, or that you believe a great many people will be interested in, then read library books and magazines on that subject, extracting the important ideas you come across. Hey, some newsletters are just a collection of press releases from companies in a specific industry and then sold to others in that industry.

Find out beforehand if others already are publishing a newsletter on the topic you have chosen. Your public library will have a reference source, or write to or email *Hudson's Newsletter Directory. the Newsletter Clearing House, 44 W. Market St. Rhinebeck, NY 12572* naming the subject you plan to write about. You don't have to have an exclusive topic, but why venture into an overcrowded field?

Advisable not to issue a stock market newsletter -- that field is overcrowded. It is important that your topic be of interest to great many people (a newsletter on "*Collecting Mason Jars*" will have a very limited audience) As one suggestion, if you are a computer-whiz you could issue a newsletter reporting on new software and devices for computer users, getting your material from newspapers and magazines and re-writing it so as not to plagiarize. Once again, the choice of a topic is the most important element in selling a Newsletter.

Newsletters sell anywhere from $49 to $450 for 12 issues. What would you pay for one titled "*Locations of Forgotten Gold Mines*" or "*Sunken Treasure Ships in America*"?

Suppose you were able to get just 100 subscribers? That's good money coming in every month (or week!)

However. getting those subscribers can be expensive unless you know how to get free publicity, easily the most effective way to reach prospective subscribers. Trying to get subscriptions by direct mail could wipe out your capital (figure on a one percent favorable response, at most).

Newsletters can be very profitable inasmuch as your costs will be for duplicating a few pieces of paper. The biggest cost is getting subscribers. After a few years, renewals will be good source of income, along with referrals. it is not a good idea to start publishing your newsletter until you have enough subscribers to make the venture viable, otherwise you will be committed to either delivering the promised number of issues or giving the few subscribers their money back.

Newsletters typically do not carry advertising, but some newsletter publishers get paid for favorable reviews or mentions -- considered by many a breach of ethics. However, you could write a newsletter for specific groups of advertisers, such as dentists, opticians, veterinarians, investment advisors, insurance agents, dentists, , etc. Its objective will be to create customers. Get your material from trade papers.

Before launching your Newsletter write a sample copy and run a "rough" issue past those whose judgments you value. Better still, get the opinion of some people in your target audience. Once again, the "topic" is the most important factor.

HANDICAP SUPPLIES STORE

Use your garage or rent a storage space that permits frequent visitors. Offer **NEW and USED** wheelchairs, scooters, lifts, adult tricycles, walkers, lift chairs -- all types of equipment and supplies needed by the aged and handicapped, even canes and crutches. Check Yellow Pages to see what competition there is, if any. Get most of your equipment on consignment from present owners (on 60-40 or 50-50 basis) You can often can buy items at low prices from spouse of those just deceased. Location is not very important for this business, so get lowest cost space you can find until your business is thriving. Some people get a new scooter (motorized wheel chair) at little or no cost because federal government subsidizes cost, so don't carry many of this item or buy one outright unless it is almost a give-away. Visit NEW-equipment sellers to find out going prices for various, new items and to find out how Medicare provides scooters. Also, the stores may be willing to sell their trade-in items to you?

If there are several new-equipment stores who also sell used handicap equipment that may be tough competition. *Try to sell used equipment at half-price or less while still charging double your cost.* If you presently are employed, you could open your "store" only on weekends, take phone calls during the week from those inquiring whether you have a specific item in stock?

Notes on this business:

WEEKEND USED-VEHICLE SALES LOT

Find a large lot on a main road you can rent at a low price for use just on Saturday and Sunday, perhaps for two hundred dollars at most (could be an out-parcel in a shopping center. A former used-car lot is ideal). Then run a large display ad in the Thursday, Friday and Saturday newspaper or (better) distribute "under the wiper" circulars offering a place for vehicle owners (cars, trucks, SUV's, rec vehicles, etc) to sell their vehicle themselves on the weekend. The ad should emphasize this is a great way for Buyers to get a vehicle below dealer prices, a great way for Sellers to reach a lot of Buyers (The Display Advertising department of the newspaper will help you write effective copy with a good lay-out, but try circulars first ($25 per 1000)

Sellers should pay (say) $50 to get admission to the lot, $75 for trucks and large vehicles. Used car dealers may want to display a vehicle or two. That's O.K. in the start-up phase but for you to decide on later whether you want to admit dealers. They should not dominate on the lot, in any case.

The selling could start at 9 A.M. and end at 4 P.M.(There will be early-birds). You don't care what the vehicles sell for. The only money you make is the $50-$75 for each "For sale" vehicle you get on lot. Give Sellers your paste-on sticker for the windshield, so you know the vehicle on display was paid for (some sellers may try to sneak their vehicle onto the lot).

You should encourage sellers to put the price and model year on the windshield (have windshield markers available for their use.) If vehicle is not sold on Saturday you could offer next day re-admission for (say) $25.

You could get vehicle transfer forms from the Department of Motor Vehicles (if needed), give one to Sellers as a courtesy. You also could have book of Deposit Receipts and give a copy to each Seller. They will need to give a receipt when taking a deposit.

A local bank or finance company may be interested in having a representative on the lot to take finance applications. Contact them. (the Rep can use a folding card table with a sign on it). This will be a big plus to attract more Sellers and Buyers. You also could arrange for special low price at nearest car wash place, so Sellers can have clean vehicle (Give Sellers a wash card when they sign up). In short, make it a business that provides services to Buyers and Sellers. What you should aim for is a large selection of vehicles and a large number of buyers. Suppose you get 100 cars every Saturday and Sunday? That's adds up to over $5000 - a decent income after deducting lot rental cost and advertising cost. And suppose you eventually get 200 vehicles on display and a big crowd of Buyers? Do the arithmetic. The income can be big.

SELLING GOVERNMENT PUBLICATIONS

The U.S. government publishes over 60,000 titles a year covering almost every conceivable subject, from bee farming (honey) to fish farming, to How to Raise Hackles or raise a herd of naugas (for naugahides). Seriously, you can make money selling these booklets because you can get them free and photocopy them without infringement on copyrights (goes for all government publications).

Get a list of titles from U.S. Government Printing Office and pick out the one's you believe will sell in your area. For example, there are booklets explaining how the government finances new businesses. There are hundreds of booklets on agricultural practices and on running a business.   One place to start is by writing for catalog from: Superintendent of Documents, U.S. Government Printing Office, Washington, DC 20402.

How much should you sell the booklets for? -- anywhere from $1 (plus postage) to $5, depending upon length and popularity of the subject. Advertise several titles in a classified ad or on the Internet. (You do not have to mention they are government booklets) The government is glad to get more circulation for their booklets and hopes you make a lot of money selling them. Some retail stores may want to buy copies from you to give away to their customers if the booklets will increase their sales. For example, a booklet "*How to lay bathroom tiles*" can increase sales for home-supply stores.

A booklet "Best way to finance a house purchase" can increase business for real estate agents Sell them in quantity at twice your cost for businesses to give away to prospective customers.

For booklet titles you also could write to U.S. Printing Office, *Consumer Booklets, Pueblo, Colorado 81001*

HOME CLEANING SERVICES

These days when both husband and wife usually have outside jobs the need for housecleaning services is high. It is not difficult to get clients who will pay $8 to $10 per hour and up (depending upon economic conditions in your area). But to make a really good income you will have to hire others to service clients you can't handle yourself because you already are too busy. (Hire them as Independent Contractors).

Locating good, dependable workers who have their own car can be a headache. It is easy to get into this business because it requires only a small investment for cleaning materials. Consequently in some towns and cities the competition can be fierce. Still, as in any business, superior customer service will win out.

You can get office cleaning jobs if you or your workers can work at night. Retail stores also use after-hours cleaning services (floor polishing often required). Don't overlook hospitals and clinics and medical profession offices doctors, dentists, opticians, etc.

You may have to obtain a bond to protect against stealing of valuables by the hired help. Check out cost with an insurance agent. Try to hire only long-time residents and home owners. Women usually are best at house cleaning.

Cleaning of windows and blinds can be lucrative specialty. Don't overlook restaurants as possible clients. Their kitchen must be cleaned every night (because of possible Board of Health inspection at any time). One couple we heard about earns $90,000 a year cleaning restaurant kitchens exclusively.

Cleaning is a low-entry cost business that can be built into a big-time operation, producing income while you and spouse take a two-weeks' cruise or other deluxe vacation.

Notes on this business:

ADVENTURE TRAVEL AND TOURS

This business not only can produce a nice income but also give you the fun of traveling with groups to exotic places. The major investment will be in advertising and promotion to form groups for travel to places like Alaska, Africa, South America - other exotic locations. You can charge (say) $200 over single travel rate (but when you match up compatible people for room accommodations, the price you charge them will be less than a single traveling alone). Once you have a group of (say) ten or more people you can make special arrangements (get a discounted price) with hotels, airlines, buses, etc.

Traveling with a group is fun for a lot of people, especially if you tailor the group so It has Interests In common (college grads, singles, church members, seniors, all women, all men, same political party, etc.) The Tour Guide should be a fun-loving person yet able to win respect and exercise authority. Travel can be by bus, train, or by air or cruise ship (or tramp steamer) river rafting, etc.

Bus tours also can be organized. You pick out an interesting destination   (gambling places, scenic locations, race tracks, historical places (like Charlestown, South Carolina or gold mining towns, Cape Canaveral, etc.) and hire a bus that has a toilet. Usually, the destination should be reached in less than five hours, unless you arrange motel accommodations for longer trips. If you can supply music for group sing-a-longs during the bus ride that's a plus. You should strive to create a fun and friendly atmosphere, so people enjoy meeting others on the trip.

Some States may require a travel agent license, most don't for this type of operation. Post notices on the bulletin boards of all the condominium developments in your area. Senior citizens are prime prospects for travel and tours. This is a great business for someone who likes to travel, is able to do so because of not being tied down and enjoys being the center of attention. Very important, it can produce good income on top of high-style living. How do you get off to a good start? -- see "Sales Promotion" section. Also, there is a Tour Guide Association and several travel magazines you can scan to get ideas for interesting guided tours you can offer in your area.

Check our "Recommended Books" section.

TUTORING SERVICE

Run a classified ad or put a notice on teachers' bulletin boards at various schools to locate teachers willing to do tutoring in spare time. You also can use college grads. Run an ad in newspaper offering one-on-one tutoring service in such subjects as Reading and Arithmetic, foreign languages, etc.   Also put notice on public bulletin boards at supermarkets, laundromats, etc. Also, offer help with students' homework.

Charge by the hour ($15 to $20). You usually can use public library for one-on-one tutoring and many schools will permit on-site tutoring after school hours, until 5 P.M. or 6 P.M. (when custodian leaves). Charge a lower price for group tutoring (Kids will learn to read fast when they can pronounce the sound each letter makes. They must come to realize that, just as in music notation, each letter (not just vowels) is a symbol for a sound). You could advertise that if child does not read well after (x) hours, tuition will be refunded (Does not apply to mentally handicapped). This can be a profitable and satisfying business that can be started for a couple hundred dollars.

You also could offer computer tutoring (Search bookstore and public library for helpful books on tutoring in general).

This is not an activity for someone who is impatient or who has no real interest in helping others. It calls for patience, a desire to help children and others to experience the joys of learning and being capable in a subject. Don't hire or keep tutors lacking the personal characteristics needed to make learning a joyful experience. They can hurt rather than help. You also can offer tutoring in other fields: languages, golf, speaking, writing, etc.

(See best book on tutoring).

HOME-MADE FOOD ITEMS

This kind of business takes lots of time, energy, and dirty work (cleaning up). Even if you bake the best cookies (or whatever) in your State if you have to limit your sales to friends and neighbors the odds are *against* your making a steady income. To make money with a home-made, food product you will need <u>wholesale</u> buyers who order on a regular basis --such as restaurants, delicatessens, hotels, roadside stands, etc. To establish such connections you usually must offer free samples to prospective outlets. If they take-on your product you will need to boost their sales of your item by providing an attractive small sign or other means for getting their patrons' attention. Don't put a price on sign! That's for outlet to decide.

Avoid items that go stale in a day or two. The outlet will expect you to collect stale items and credit them with the cost of the item. Your wholesale selling price needs to be calculated very carefully. Retail outlets want at least 25 percent profit.

Some sellers are doing well with refrigerated items, and with home-made lollipops, brownies, pies, cakes, cookies, peppermint patties, jams, jellies, candles, etc.

You should look into license requirements. The Board of Health may require a physical exam and a regular inspection of your premises. Look into the possibility of using the kitchen in a church, clubhouse, condominium, or other seldom-used facility. They may be receptive to your using their kitchen in exchange for a small rent or for supplying your specialty for the functions they hold on occasion.

Before you invest money to produce a large quantity of your specialty, hand out samples to friends, acquaintances, and potential outlets to get their reaction. If you don't get a clear playback of (honest) approval and encouragement, your product won't stay the course. Either improve it or give up the idea. Not everyone can duplicate the history of Pepperidge Farms which started with one woman baking a few loaves of bread for friends. Come to think of it, almost everyone who has traveled abroad comes back realizing that almost all breads in America are inferior to those in Europe, including those turned out today by Pepperidge Farms. The reason probably is that American breads are made to keep "fresh" for about a week. How? -by using chemicals. That's why taste of "home-made products" often is superior. *See related book in "Recommended Books" section.*

CATERING

Caterers are used at wedding receptions, business parties, bar mitzvahs, corporate functions, social club celebrations, etc. The biggest challenge is getting customers-- because most of those who hire a caterer will go by recommendations from others. Still, as in all businesses, success is won by providing superior products and services - -good food and top grade service at reasonable prices-- and by creating a good impression among the guests. This may mean having the servers wear sparkling clean, white uniforms and a perpetual smile. You should have contacts with strolling musicians and keyboard players if background music is wanted.

You do not necessarily have to be a good cook. Usually, hors d'ouevres (finger foods) are served during the cocktail phase before dinner. (these can be bought from upscale delicatessens). The host has to decide whether meal will be served as a sit-down, a waited-on meal, or in cafeteria style (much less expensive). If you are providing the food consider *buying* what you need -- whole barbeque chickens or fried-chicken pieces from a local supermarket (wholesale basis).

You can buy other food items from fast-food outlets or from restaurants (on special order). Baked potatoes are good for sit-down meals, not for cafeteria-style meals (use potato salad, other foods not requiring use of knife). Asparagus adds class to a meal. A good dessert can save a lack-luster meal. Ice cream with butterscotch or chocolate topping is an excellent dessert. But for food planning and needed equipment (coffee/tea urns, bowls, etc.) you should read a book on catering.

Catering as a business works best when there are several members of a family who can be called upon when needed.

To get customers, put a business card on bulletin boards and personally leave one at bridal shops and meeting halls. Look in the local newspaper for notices of weddings, engagements, and upcoming functions, and mail a circular extolling your ability to serve food "just right" for the kind of people who will be attending the function, from "very classy" to "very economical, yet satisfying to all." This can be a good, part-time business that eventually could be built-up into a high income producer. However, it takes a lot of hard work, just as does a restaurant. This is not an easy business to run.

(Look for the "Best Book" on catering in our "Books" index).

COURIER SERVICE

Use your vehicle to deliver letters, documents, small packages, etc., locally. Get customers by putting notices on bulletin boards and by delivering a circular to businesses, offices, secretarial services, etc. Get competitive rates by phoning other courier services (price usually depends upon distance and on urgency). When very busy use others to make deliveries with their vehicle, hiring them as an Independent Contractor, not as employees.(*See Independent Contract Agreement form in Index*) You will need answering machine to take messages at all hours (turn ringer off at night).

Some individuals who started with their own vehicle, now have fleet of courier vehicles (usually small vans). Contact your auto insurance agent to make sure you have proper insurance protection.

You also could offer to make airport runs to deliver or pick up packages or incoming passengers. Another source of revenue is delivering meals for restaurants. Contact the expensive places (not pizza parlors) to make an arrangement.

Check to see what the local competition is and inquire about rates. Don't worry if others are in this business. Would you be afraid to open a used car business because there already is one in town ? The essence of the entrepreneurial drive is to be the best place in town --not to seek a monopoly. If you own a reliable car, you can get into the courier business with $25 worth of circulars distributed around your area or town. It may take several months before you are earning over $100-$200 a week -- but it might not! You could earn that much within a short time. However, this is a good business for a single man without a lot of fixed expenses or for a semi-retired Senior.

Dress appropriately for your services -- a uniform often gives impression of professionalism. Avoid imprinted, white T-shirts--that's underwear.

Check newspapers and yellow pages to see how much competition exists and prices being charged. Call on stores and companies to tell them about your courier and package delivery and airport services. Leave a card or circular. You may need to increase your automobile insurance to "commercial" status when appropriate.

Notes on this business:

CHAUFFEURING

Use your vehicle (if it is an appropriate one) to drive people to airports, train stations, shopping expeditions, assist aged to their appointments, to church, funerals, weddings, etc. It is like a taxi service, but more elegant.

You could wear a chauffeur cap, act like a chauffeur -- opening the door, assisting people in and out, handling the packages or luggage, waiting for client to return. etc. You could develop a list of regular customers who you serve on a schedule.

Your vehicle should be kept sparkling clean inside and out, perhaps with occasional use of air freshener (altho some make car smell like a toilet). Your fee usually will be on hourly basis ($12 up). You should be available on short notice, day or night, so a cell phone is almost a necessity. You may need to upgrade your driver's license --not difficult. You also can rent a limousine for special occasions Try the local funeral homes as a possible source of limousines for rent for evening affairs (funerals usually take place during daylight hours).

Get business with small classified ad under "Personals". A large part of your income will come from referrals by satisfied customers who recommend you to friends and business associates. Look and act like the chauffeurs you see in the movies. People love being catered to. With you it's a job.

Notes on this business:

VIDEO INTRODUCTIONS

Many newspapers and Internet sites find it very profitable to run a full page of ads by men and women seeking a relationship. Contacts are by phone costing $2 to $4 a minute. This procedure usually results in a great many, disappointing, "blind dates." It is much more effective when seeking a suitable person for a relationship if you can see and hear those who also are seeking a relationship. That's why with "Video Dating" you can make money.

You can buy a used digital camcorder costing as little as $300 (Sony is best) or rent one. You will need a tripod (about $25). Use a solid color background (a wide black or dark blue shade (about $25) and some auxiliary lighting (about $70), some videotape (about $2 a roll) and you are equipped for the video-dating business. Now the question is where to do this? Your garage, or rental of a neighbor's, can be turned into a studio, as can your family-room (all visits are by appointment). Or you may find a small office to rent on month-to-month basis at a low rent.

You charge a fee ($15 - $25) to do a three-minute (say) video and voice recording, and you charge a fee ($10 - $20) for anyone who wants to view these videos. Clients who are videotaped should give a phone number only. Some clients may not want to have anyone contact them for a date until they see a videotape of those asking for that date ($5 charge) To get clients you can run a small, classified ad under "Personals" or a continuous one-inch display ad until your service is well known. Put a business card on bulletin boards everywhere.

This can be a fun business, especially for a single person. If you are married it could cause trouble. The investment is a few hundred dollars. The most difficult part is editing the videos. This can be farmed out until you learn how to do it yourself.

MAKE BIG BUCKS HELPING HOMELESS AND UNEMPLOYED PEOPLE

Contact a church or social service organization needing money. Offer to share with them the proceeds from sales of donated books (hardcover only). Then contact city manager for permission to let the homeless or unemployed sell the books at $1 each on street corners with high, pedestrian traffic. Then get the local newspaper to run a story about the project, citing need for donating (hardcover) books to the sponsoring church or organization (which arranges for a book drop-off place). No retail license needed - books are "free speech."

The book sellers get 50 cents per book sold, the sponsoring organization gets 25 cents per book and you get 25 cents per book. Average sales per bookseller should be about 40 books a day (some more, some less), giving homeless $20 a day or about $120 a week -- enough for a room and meals, taking them off the street at night.

Let's say you arrange for ten locations. With an average of 40 books sold per location per day (times six days) the sponsoring organization and you will get about $100 a day or $600 a week.

To earn your "cut" you will have to locate suitable homeless persons willing to do this (some towns and cities have "Homeless" agencies). Arrange for each Seller to get 200 books per day for display in an open, rented trailer or in portable bookcases made by members of the sponsoring organization. There are other details, but you now have the essentials of this worthwhile and profitable business (which can be done at same time in surrounding towns). This is a case of making money while doing something good for your fellow-man and the community.

SELL PRODUCTS WHILE YOU SLEEP

You can buy a telephone answering machine today for about $50 to $79 that has one or more "mail boxes" which will deliver separate sales messages when the caller pushes a "menu" button. That phone should permit you to record an outgoing sales message 1-3 minutes long and to record at least 15 minutes of incoming messages. And it helps if the phone has "caller I.D." (as a back-up).

The separate business" mailbox" enables personal calls to still come in and be answered individually.

Now you need a product to sell. It could be books with wide appeal (usually self-help books), magazine subscriptions, discount restaurant booklets (buy one meal, get 50 percent off on additional meal), an Internet- connection service, an Introduction Service--any unique products on which you earn several dollars without having to stock the item (products could be drop shipped by supply -source to whom you furnish shipping labels).

Now, very important, you will need a persuasive sales message that is delivered when someone phones and selects the sales number on the menu.

Keep improving that message, possibly getting help from the product supplier who may also let you use their credit card service.

How do you get calls? - by running a small, classified ad on a continuous basis, by posting a message on bulletin boards, using circulars put under car wiper blades, etc. You do not need to answer the phone. At night simply turn the ringer off. The machine still will take messages.

When you leave the house make sure the answering machine is set to take messages. In this way you can make sales without ever talking to prospective buyers -- the recorded sales message should make sales for you. At end of sales message it should ask for caller's name, address and phone number, so you can confirm order and credit card data before arranging shipping. Hey, how easier can it get? If you don't have a pleasant voice, get someone to record the message for you. Once again, the sales message has to be persuasive. Keep refining it, so it becomes more and more effective.

SELLING PETS FROM HIGHWAY HOMES

People who live on busy highways provide an outlet for high priced, product sales. For example, you can sell many puppies every day by giving two of them to participating home owners who live on a busy highway and will permit a small sign out front, such as "Poodle Puppies For Sale."

The puppies should be American Kennel Club (AKC) registered, not mixed breeds (Mongrels can be obtained for nothing at city-run animal shelters).The puppies could sell from $100 to $300, depending upon breed (Golden Retrievers, German Shepherds, and Australian sheep dogs, and small lap-dogs, for example, fetch a high price). The home owner could get (say) $25 for each sale (and in many cases will buy one of the puppies because of becoming attached to it).

You will have to make connections with dog breeders to get a steady supply of healthy puppies (See dog publications and look up "Dog Breeders" on the Internet).   Suppose you sign up ten highway homes which sell an average of three puppies a week. If you make $50 per puppy that's $1500 a week for you, less cost of small signs (should look home-made), shipping costs, and automobile expenses. And suppose you had 20 outlets?

There are other items ideal for selling from highway homes (Give this some thought). They should involve a selling price that enables you to give the home owner an incentive to participate (perhaps earnings of at least $100 a month) and gives you a profit of at least $25 to $50 per sale. Because of zoning restrictions the item being sold should not create the aspects of a regular business -- that's why puppies are ideal. However, many highway-located homes will be zoned for commercial activity and can obtain a business license at low cost. These business-zoned homes legally can sell any product permitted by the zoning regulations. Can you think of another product to sell this way, besides puppies? Kittens may be okay if they are scarce breeds, like Siamese and Persian and other exotics, but they will fetch only $100 or so. Still, kittens may sell faster because of lower prices than puppies. The basic idea is to turn highway homes into retail outlets, producing income for you and the home owner.

SMALL ENGINE REPAIR

If you have some mechanical ability and can get balky, small engines running smoothly you can turn your garage or a storage space into a small-engine repair shop.   There are lots of people with cranky lawn-mowers, blowers, generators, and other small, gasoline engines, who need repair help. You could charge $20 to $35 an hour, charging highest rate for repairing outboard motors.

You could run a continuous, small classified ad, such as *"Small gasoline engines repaired. Your place or mine.   Work guaranteed. John Smith, Phone 000-0000"*

There are more and more small engines being used -- for scooters, pressure washers, blowers, chain saws, etc.   Don't worry about not being an expert. There are books available on the subject. If you have some tools, a place to work, can obtain parts, you can be working full-time or part-time in a few weeks -- unless you can't   change a faucet washer. Yes, it takes *some* mechanical ability - and a couple hundred dollars for ads and/or circulars, a work bench and some tools. Properly handled, your small, gas engine repair business could grow so fast you'll soon be advertising for a helper. (*See Sales Promotion section - also the "Recommended Book" on small engine repair*).

Notes on this business:

RECORDING SPEECHES

If you live in a city having several hotels and motels with meeting rooms, contact the managers to find out which companies or groups have scheduled a meeting (You also can get this information from business magazines at the library). Email or write to those companies or groups, offering to do a professional recording of the speeches **without charge** if they will give you a mailing list of members or personnel NOT attending who could be interested in buying an audiocassette of the speeches for $10 to $20 (price depends upon length of list). The company also may want to buy several cassettes. You also can record speeches by politicians and by celebrities visiting your city, and offer the recordings to supporters and fans for $10 or more, perhaps giving political organization or sponsors a small percentage (if necessary).

If you don't have a professional audio recorder you can rent one on day needed (best, a Nagra). You also will need a good microphone with long arm-attachment.

This same procedure can be used for video taping, (*See "Video Recording" business*) but to avoid a static, speech-numbing video you should include other activities at the meeting or convention, such as parties, softball game, golfing, etc.

In both cases you will need to do some editing. You also can sell your audio and video recording services outright to meeting planners and organizations for an agreed-upon flat fee. Again, rented equipment is ideal for start-up purposes.

You may need help with editing of audio and videotapes. Buy that help until you know how to do editing yourself.

Your notes on this business:

PAINTING JOBS

Most important part of painting of houses, interiors, garages, fences, etc. is to get jobs on a steady basis, so you will have a steady income. Now, you may not be a skilled painter, but how much skill does it take to paint fences, doors, kitchen cabinets, and other easy jobs? You will learn fast. It is not advisable to take on the job of painting the exterior of a house if you haven't done it before. Better to start with inside, interior paint jobs where you can use a roller and a step ladder. Today, there are tools that make it easy to paint ceilings, windows, and other erstwhile difficult surfaces. Painters easily can get $25 an hour and up.

When you are ready to paint houses you can rent the equipment you need --ladders, scaffolds, pressure cleaners, drop cloths, tarps, spray guns, etc. You will need help for this kind of job. College guys are a good source of temp labor, but it is better to have someone you can call upon on a regular basis. Be advised that in many States it is necessary to get a license (if you are going to advertise yourself as a professional painter).

If you want jobs painting houses, the best way to get them is to walk around looking for houses that badly need a coat of paint. Knock on the door and offer to give them a quote. If they say they can't afford it, remind them that they may qualify for a low-cost loan against their equity which can be paid off over several years.

There is plenty of painting work at all times. If you don't want to do the painting yourself, get the jobs and hire others to do the painting. That's what is called "entrepreneurial drive."

Start this business for under $250. Look into "Wagner" power painting equipment and get their helpful training booklets. Your local public library may have "How To" books on painting techniques, as well as on other businesses described in this book. (*See our book list*)

SECRETARIAL SERVICES

Individuals and one-person companies frequently need to have letters, envelopes, reports, manuscripts, etc. typed neatly. It helps if you have a computer, but a high-grade electric typewriter may do (You can buy a used IBM Selectric today for about $40, or (better) a used word-processor for about $50

Get customers by running a continuous 3-line classified ad, preferably under "Personals." Also, put notices on bulletin boards all over town. Try to get a notice posted about your services in those stores that rent mailboxes (Mailboxes Etc., Pak-Mail, and other chains). The boxes usually are rented by one-person businesses which often need secretarial help.

If you want to do it, emphasize your willingness to handle bulk, direct mailings. This involves making a great many copies of an approved letter, typing addresses on letters and envelopes or buying a mailing list on self-stick mailing labels, sealing envelopes and putting on stamps.

With frequent jobs, you may want to go to the Post Office and get a Bulk-Mailing Permit which lowers stamp costs on 200 pieces or more. Also contact printing shops to arrange for a commission on any printing jobs you bring in (as a Broker). However, copy machines today can do a great job for about three cents a copy or less (100 or more copies).Use a better copy paper when called for, as for instance, when copying letterheads.

Depending upon economic conditions in your area, you can charge $15 to $20 an hour or $3 per double-spaced page of a report or manuscript (a good typist can do 7 to 9 pages an hour). Some libraries have free use of computers and permit limited "print" use. One might be used for an occasional job. When promoting your business you could offer "Proof Reading Service" if you are able to scan text quickly and spot typos. Companies also use outside secretarial services during work overloads. Send them a circular.

(See "Recommended Books" section)

TRANSLATION SERVICES

If you speak and write a foreign language, offer to do translations in that language for businesses, hotels lawyers, police and sheriff departments, courts, and individuals. Also, locate others who also speak and write a different language (Could be local individuals or those found on the Internet) and also sell their services. Accurate translations are worth $50 an hour and up, depending upon scarcity of others who also can translate that language (Spanish translators are easy to find, command less money; those who can translate Chinese, Japanese, Arabic, or other exotic languages will command highest rates). Today, many public corporations want their annual and quarterly reports and sales literature translated Into Spanish. This activity alone could yield an annual income of over $50,000.

Interestingly, it now is possible to buy computer software that will translate many languages, including some not often encountered. You could have this software available to help individuals and companies who get an occasional foreign letter in a language you also are unacquainted with or those who want to send a letter in the language of an intended foreign recipient.

Chinese, Japanese, and Arabic translators are in big demand, can get a high price for their translation services.

All it takes is some advertising and promotion and perhaps some language translation software. An ideal part-time business, it will grow as you get referrals from clients. You also will meet some people born in same country as you or your parents and could take part in some interesting foreign matters. Not wise to attempt this business if you have only a few years of U.S. schooling. Some of the English words will be "foreign" to you.

(See "Recommended books").

MINDING PETS

If you have a fenced yard (and tolerant neighbors) you could offer to mind pets (usually a dog or cat) for owners who work all day and have no one at home to take care of the pet. Also, people who go on vacation or business trips need a place to take care of their pet. This is a business only for those who like animals, who are not afraid of dogs and other pets. The animals could be kept on a long leash that permits movement but prevents escape or fighting. Rain cover may be necessary. You also could use your garage or carport.

People will pay $10 to $20 a day for minding a pet from (say) 8.A.M. to 6 P.M., more if kept overnight (Check prices asked by local kennels - they vary depending upon economic condition of area. Obviously you can get higher price in San Francisco than in East Snowshoe, Maine).

If a pet looks sick, refuse to take it in because it may be contagious for other animals in your care. Make sure the veterinarians in town know about your service. You may be a good referral source for them.

Your goal should be to take in at least $60 a day in this business. It is a business, however, that requires many hours of someone's time, and perhaps weekends. It is ideal for someone of advanced years obliged to stay at home for some reason, but not particularly good if you have small children .

(See "Promotion" section of this manual for tips on building your business; also "Pet Care" book)

CARPET CLEANING

This is a highly competitive business because it is so easy to enter. However, you can make $100 or more a day just from three or four jobs that take little more than an hour each. You can rent a professional carpet cleaning machine from a Rental Equipment store or a lesser one at the supermarket. To do a better job than most competitors in the carpet-cleaning biz use a rented rotating-brush, professional floor machine, as opposed to the usual wand that wets the carpet and sucks the water back up seconds later (Some dirt needs to be soaked for a minute or more to loosen it and then a rotating brush to force it away from the carpet strands). The ideal rotating-brush machine will have a suction attachment, but you can use a standard rotating-brush machine and then use a powerful wet-vacuum (not the $39 type found in home improvement and hardware stores). In short, do a superior job and you won't have to worry about all the competition almost all of which use wands.

Check local prices before advertising or quoting yours. You do not have to be the cheapest. Tip: stay away from oriental rug cleaning. And you will need to be careful about the cleaning chemicals you use. Some cheap ones will fade the color of carpeting or cause other problems. Stick with top-name brands that have a warranty, Wall-to-wall carpeting can cost several thousands of dollars and could cost you that much if you ruin someone's expensive carpeting, particularly by getting it so wet it shrinks the carpet. Your public library may have books on carpet cleaning. Makers of cleaning machines and suppliers of chemicals also will have free, training booklets.

(See "Promotion" section for ideas on building this business and "Recommended Books" section).

USED CLOTHING STORE

So-called "thrift" stores are being opened at a fast pace all over the country. And if times get worse, with high unemployment, more and more people will start buying their clothing (even shoes) from thrift stores. Problem is, this is a very competitive business even right now. Aside from several new stores opening up every month, there usually is competition from the religious sects, from the Salvation Army, Good-Will, VNA, and other such organizations --and they get their clothing without cost. If you don't have these competitors in your area you are lucky.

Without an organization in back of you where are you going to get the used clothing you need? Many thrift stores buy their inventory from the Salvation Army, Good-Will, and such places because the prices are so low that they can be marked-up and still be a bargain. But buy only like-new clothing.

Most thrifts get their clothing, especially children's clothing, on consignment (50-50 or 60-40) or buy outright from parents or allow them to swap (plus 25 percent) for larger sizes as the kids grow up. If in a small town, you may have to get your inventory from a nearby city, buying from charitable thrift stores.

All clothing you take in should be freshly washed or dry-cleaned before offering it to the public. (Try to make an arrangement with a dry-cleaner for a special low-price). Some stores specialize in expensive dresses and coats that can be sold for a fraction of their original selling price (usually obtained on consignment). For such stores it is almost a necessity to have a seamstress available to do low-cost alterations. Same thing can be done with men's suits, altho these don't sell as fast. Men's clothing usually is obtained from widows, so some proprietors scan the obituaries every day. They buy only seldom-worn suits, pay only $5 to $15 for them. A man's suit originally costing $150 or more can be sold for $25 to $50, depending upon its quality.

You could run a thrift store out of your living room or suitably-decorated garage. Racks can be made from PVC pipe and put on castors so they can be wheeled out of sight when entertaining "company" or relatives *(See "Gown Rentals")*.

Keep in mind you will be dealing mostly with budget-minded customers who often are scrimping in order to make ends meet. Don't get upset by those inclined toward haggling. Your prices should permit a little discounting. Remember old Chinese saying "*Person without smile should not open shop.*"

MAKING WOOD PRODUCTS AT HOME

Use your garage or basement or a rented storage bay to cut and assemble wood items that will sell for a good price (not toys or small items). For example, you could produce sturdy work-tables, or benches, saw-horses, dog houses, playground items such as overhead ladders that kids love to swing on, etc. One need not be an expert cabinet maker, but if you can make custom-built cabinets for doctors, dentists, and other professionals you could keep busy year-round. Making wood items for sale can be satisfying and profitable, but you must concentrate on higher-price items. Cheap wooden pieces easily are mass-produced in China and Mexico. Their shipping costs on big items can help you outprice them.

Caution: Don't go hog-wild buying machinery. Wait until you have orders to fill based upon samples. When you come up with profitable item(s) to make, you then have to create sales *(See "Sales Promotion" section and available book on marketing wood products)* You also could farm out production to individuals who have home woodworking machines and experience. If you are going to paint your products, wear a mask and arrange to have good ventilation, or farm out the painting to a regular paint shop.

NOTES ON THIS BUSINESS:

BULK MAILING SERVICE

This is a business that can be made into a very profitable "at home" activity. Companies now send out mail at a postage cost of 37 cents each. Yet, if there are 200 or more pieces and the outgoing letters are zip coded the postage drops to about 25 cents each - a 12 cents savings or $12 per hundred. Many firms and individuals send out 100's or 1000's of letters every month. You can make money by saving them money. You'll need a bulk mailing permit for $300 and zip coding software plus a (rented) postal meter to print postage and you are in business. You can charge 50 percent of the savings involved.

Also, you could offer to maintain mailing lists for clients or obtain appropriate lists for those seeking to sell something. Ask $25 an hour.

You also can offer to send invitations and greeting cards. Then you can offer to put mailing labels on envelopes, fold and insert the letter and any inserts. In short, you can offer a complete mailing service, in many towns much needed.

A one-inch ad in a business newspaper will bring in customers as will a circular dropped off at offices and at mail centers which rent boxes (Boxes mostly are rented by one-person businesses which often need mailing help). Check yellow pages to see how much competition exists. Also make inquiries at your local post office(s) to check on competition. Chances are there isn't much.   You can run this business from the dining room table and members of family will enjoy helping with the folding, inserting, etc.

Just make sure the letters going out don't have peanut butter and jelly on them.

NOTES ON THIS BUSINESS:

AUTOMOBILE "DETAILING"

The word "detailing" means cleaning and polishing every detail of the vehicle -- right up to polishing the rim around the dome light and vacuuming the ash trays in the rear. In short the service being offered is to make a vehicle as new-looking as possible. This includes washing the car by hand (many owners do not like the stiff brushes in automatic car washes), using a soft brush to clean the brake-dust from the wheels, and even using Q-tips to clean the crevices on the dashboard. The vehicle then is vacuumed and polished with a high-grade polish (several are excellent and easy to apply and remove). When you can afford it you may want to use an electric buffer (about $75).

Your clients will be owners of expensive cars who don't mind paying $50-up for a first-class detailing job. In California, fussy car owners will pay $300 and up for superior detailing.

This is not a business likely to succeed in a small town or one hard-hit with unemployment. It is a good business for someone who is a car enthusiast and who takes pleasure in making a vehicle look its best.

Some used-car dealers will pay a good fee to have their better cars detailed. *New* car dealers usually have their own detailing shop.

You can use your garage or driveway or rent a storage space to do the work and may offer to do the work at the client's house or business location. Some detailers in warm-weather areas work outside and use a simple 4-post, canvas awning with a large fan to keep cool. No doubt about it -- this is a business only for someone who can do hard work -- or hire people to do it. Best part -- it takes very little money to start. Best way to get customers is to put a circular under wipers of cars in shopping centers. Offer a "special" get-acquainted price or package to build a customer following.

CONTINUAL GARAGE SALES

People love to attend garage sales looking for bargains and unusual items. You can hold a garage sale every weekend or, if employed, maybe every two weeks, using one week- end to go around to other garage sales looking for items you can buy at a very low price and resell at your own garage sales. You also can pick up bargains at charity-run thrift stores and used-furniture stores.

If you don't have a suitable garage, look into a using a low-cost. shade-cover for automobiles that can easily be erected in your backyard or driveway and quickly taken down, perhaps drilling holes for the support poles. This will work only in mild weather and not on windy days.

You also could hold a garage sale in an easy-to-locate storage facility that permits retailing, storing your items there until sale-day. The weather on your garage-sale day will play an important part in your sales volume.

If making garage sales a business, try to offer unusual items, staying away from dishes, clothing, large pieces of furniture needing two men to move.

Books take up valuable space and usually will fetch only 50 cents or a dollar at most (pay only 20 cents for hardcovers). Offer small tables, figurines, unusual, old jewelry, vases, silk flowers and trees, framed pictures, small appliances, stainless steel pots, fold-away beds, and other items that can be carried away by buyers and stowed in a car.

This is an ideal business for a couple if one of them is unemployed and so, has time to go around looking for items to resell. Your objective should be to obtain items on which you will make several dollars. To guide your own purchases ask yourself whether the item(s) you are considering will sell for at least twice what you pay for them? Keep eyes open for antiques and valuable art.

Your investment could be only a $200 or so. Rent tables needed for display, altho folding tables are inexpensive. On a good-weather day you could net $200 or more.

My notes on this business:

DRIVEWAY REPAIR SERVICE

If you keep your eyes open when driving around you will find that a great many driveways need repair, that many of them have potholes, places that are crumbling, and the ground underneath showing through. Also, many driveways are oil stained and so, detract from appearance of the property. There's a lot of money to be made cleaning, repairing and resurfacing driveways.

You will need to get acquainted with patching materials available at Home Depot, Lowe's, and other such stores. They also have booklets and clinics which tell you how to make driveway repairs. You also can get a lot of useful info from equipment rental stores. To do resurfacing you will need to rent applicators and rollers and/or pressure cleaners.. But, hey, someone with a little mechanical ability should be able to quickly learn how to make good repairs. Concrete driveways require more skill and should be avoided until you acquire the needed know-how.

Most of your customers will be home owners, but you can look forward to growing your business so that you can take on parking lots, tennis courts, and other large jobs, some requiring striping. You then will be a "Paving Contractor."

Home owners easily can get a loan to pay for improvement of their driveway. Your earnings may be $25 to $35 per hour after cost of materials. When selling a job try to get at least one-third down and the balance upon completion. You will need a signed contract that specifies work to be done, when to do it, and the cost of the job to the home owner. A magnetic sign on sides of your vehicle naming your business will do much to create confidence. If you dislike calling on home owners, hire a person to do it.

(See Sales Promotion ideas in this book and Independent Contractor form to be used if hiring someone on commission basis).

MOVING BUSINESS

you can rent a truck from U-haul or other truck rental places-- by the day, or by the week. Place a small ad in the local newspaper saying "Local Moving & Deliveries-- no job too big or too small" When people respond try to book the moving jobs for the same day or days, so you can rent a truck only when you need it. You also may need to rent one or more hand-trucks (the kind that uses straps) and also blankets or pads to protect furniture.

If you need help contact temporary-help agencies and the local Unemployment Office and hire by the hour or by the day.   Keep on renting the truck you need until the rental payments exceed the monthly payment for a new or used truck.

When you get a large job that requires more than one truck-- like moving an office complex-- before you commit yourself to the job make sure you will be able to get the necessary help needed for that job.

You most likely will begin by delivering one or two items -- a sofa, chairs, etc. Call on all the Thrift Stores that sell furniture and acquaint them with your moving service, same with used furniture stores. You will need business cards ($10 for 1000 at Staples using standard format).

If you are not physically able to move furniture and appliances, you could hire temporary help to drive the truck and do pick-ups and deliveries, with you as the inside man (or woman) who books the jobs and promotes the business.

Because of Federal licensing requirements you will need to confine your moving jobs to local and in-state jobs, no out-of-state moving.

Before starting your business contact town or city agencies to find out what licenses may be needed, if any? As for the prices you need to charge, make phone calls to competitors to see what they are charging. Usually movers get from $35 to $60 an hour for a truck and two men. You can start this business for a few hundred dollars, spent mostly on ads and sales promotion

(See Sales Promotion Ideas).

PRESSURE CLEANING

You can rent high-pressure cleaning equipment to clean roofs, driveways, buildings, etc. Add $20-$25 an hour to rental costs. *(Check to learn what prices competitors are asking)* Put an ad in the newspaper offering to do high-pressure cleaning (list applications) When you get responses try to group the jobs for same day, then rent the equipment needed to do the jobs involved. Your ad should include the words "No job too big or too small." If you will be cleaning roofs you will need to rent ladders and tarps (to protect foliage).You also will need to learn the cleaning fluids to use, if any. When doing slanted roofs, wear a safety belt looped to solid chimney.

If job is too big for you to handle, subcontract it out.

To get jobs you could walk around town and find drive- ways with oil stains and buildings with rust stains or roofs that need to be cleaned. Then knock on the door. You also can get good results from a printed flyer distributed around town. If you cannot or do not want to do the work yourself you can hire temp help as an "Independent Contractor"

(See sample form) Also get release for possible injuries.

You can start this business for a few hundred dollars, spent mostly on advertising (*If you need help to compose an effective small ad get help from local newspaper personnel)* There are many ways to promote a pressure cleaning business. See the section in this book titled *"Sales Promotions."*

Notes on this business:

LANDSCAPING WORK

You can rent, as needed, small bulldozers, ditch digging machines (for laying pipe, etc) and other types of equipment used on landscaping jobs. Many of your customers will be builders and developers. The building boom may last for years. There will be ditches to dig, dirt to be moved, etc.

Don't worry about not being experienced. Get the equipment rental store to teach you how to use the equipment. This a business for someone who likes to be outdoors. Check the prices being charged by others. Add your labor charge to equipment rental cost. You will need to place an ad in local newspaper, stressing "No job too small." If you prefer not to do the work, book jobs then hire Temp workers by the hour as Independent Contractor (in writing and with their personal responsibility for any injuries). Make sure they know how to use the equipment required for the job. It is a good idea to check with an insurance agent on cost of liability insurance.

If inexperienced, try to hire a helper who has lots of experience. Read books on landscaping obtained from public library or booklet racks at Home Depot, other stores. To build this business see section in this book on "Sales Promotions.

(Also see "Recommended Books" section).

Notes on this business:

PAINTING BUSINESS

You can rent ladders. scaffolds, power painting equipment, drop cloths, etc., but will need to buy brushes, rollers, other odds and ends. If not experienced, it is best to limit yourself to interior paint jobs or jobs not requiring you to climb high ladders or erect scaffolds (paint fences, garage or house doors, porches, furniture, etc.). Hey, painting is not difficult to learn how to do skillfully. Investigate the use of WAGNER POWER PAINTING EQUIPMENT and get their free training booklets.

Power painting equipment is making many jobs very easy. Painting tips also are available in library books. Don't take on wall papering unless you have had lots of experience doing it. In many States a license is needed for professional painting. You may want to avoid advertising until able to obtain license? Check with other painting contractors to see what they are charging per hour (Usually they quote "by the job"). $20 to $40 an hour is obtainable. Your per-hour rate will depend upon the prosperity of your geographic location (and this holds for almost all small businesses that charge by the hour). You could walk around town looking for houses that need painting, knock on doors, obtain jobs even if needed to be done by licensed, professional painters, collect a commission from them, but do the small jobs yourself. If you go canvassing for house painting jobs, also keep your eyes open for driveways that need to be resurfaced. Collect a commission for locating these jobs, unless you go into the business yourself of resurfacing driveways and parking lots using rented equipment. Do you begin to see that going into business yourself requires little more than ambition, imagination, a little daring, and a little capital you can afford to risk? (and, of course, good ideas such as are in this book).

See "Sales Promotion" section in this book.

LAWN CARE

You can buy a used, self-propelled lawnmower for a hundred dollars or less and it may be adequate for mowing lawns around homes. You also will need a rake, an edger. and perhaps a blower. Total investment may run about two or three hundred dollars. However, if you get jobs involving large areas to be mowed, you could rent professional equipment as needed.   This is an easy business to get into, so it usually is highly competitive.   Most people in this business develop a list of customers whose lawn needs to be mowed every two weeks or so in the warm months. In the winter months you could arrange to clean snow away from their walks and driveway and possible do trimming of hedges, bushes, and trees (without climbing). Lawn care could also include use of fertilizers, weed elimination, getting rid of brown patches, and re-seeding --all chores for which you make an extra charge. In short, you do not just mow lawns --you provide **lawn care!** --*and that's what your business card should indicate.* You will need to run a continuous small ad in the newspaper

(If you want help with ad, ask personnel at local newspaper).

This is good business for those who like to be outdoors most of the day. Try to move into it slowly if you presently are employed by working evenings and/or weekends. Your prices will depend on rates quoted by competitors - about $20 hour. Hire needed help on part-time basis, paying by the hour. Unemployment office may help you.

(See "Recommended Books" section).

Notes on this business:

ERECTING STORAGE SHEDS

Many home-supply stores (like Home Depot, Lowe's, etc.) advertise low prices on storage sheds. But, in most cases they do not erect them. If you are able and willing to erect storage sheds let the stores know and put notices on bulletin boards wherever you can find them (Wal-Mart. K-Mart, supermarkets, laundromats, etc.) You also could run a three-line classified ad on Saturdays and Sundays on a continuous basis (on contract to get lowest price). It's worth at least $99 to have a storage shed erected (may take 3-4 hours).

You could soon be erecting 3-5 a week in spare time and on weekends. Eventually, people may ask you to recommend "best buy" in storage sheds and you can begin ordering sheds from the stores or manufacturers, possibly earning another $75-$175 per shed. You will need to know how to anchor sheds against high winds and often need a helper just to hold sections while you bolt them. In some towns, a building permit is needed by the home owner to erect a shed on their property. Most ignore this until obliged to get one. You often may need to build or buy a wooden ramp for easy access to storage shed by wheeled vehicles. And you could recommend installing simple electrical connection for a light, get paid for doing this, but only if it involves a plug-in application, otherwise you are getting involved with electrical contractor work which requires a license.

(See "Sales Promotion" section about building this business)

Notes on this business:

USED FURNITURE BUSINESS

This can be a highly profitable business, can earn $50,000 to $100,000 a year. You can start selling used furniture from your garage, or rent a large bay in a public storage facility.

You can get furniture to sell by offering a consignment plan whereby owner gets 75 to 50 percent of agreed selling price.   Also, scan the "Furniture For Sale" classified ads for bargains. Offer less than asking price, explaining that you are a dealer who has to resell at a profit.

Used mattresses, box springs, headboards are good sellers (but some States prohibit sale of used bedding. Some sellers get around this by selling headboard and frame at a high price, give the mattress free). You often can get used mattresses from furniture-store delivery people who are supposed to dispose of them. They are glad to get $15-$25. Contact them. However, stained or worn out mattresses are not worth buying. Pass them up. You could use UV light to sanitize beds, but don't claim "sterilization. UV light can damage eyes.

It is not a good idea to offer beat-up furniture such as are found at Salvation Army or Good-Will or other charity-run outlets that get furniture for nothing. (You often can find good resale items there). Offer a better class of furniture than they do. Don't buy upholstered furniture that needs to be cleaned or furniture that requires major repairs; too much time and trouble involved. Use furniture cleaners, scratch removers and fabric fresheners to add appeal to your inventory.

Advertise in newspapers that you buy furniture at fair prices. You will get calls from those wanting to sell some or all the furniture in a house or condo just bought or inherited. It usually doesn't pay to drive to Sellers having just one or two pieces to sell. Ask them to bring in the furniture or a sample chair or cushion.

This is a business that requires two people --two needed to move furniture around, one to mind store as other goes out to make bids on furniture offered for sale.

The mark-up on furniture is at least 100 percent So, if you buy something for $100 ask yourself first if it will sell for $200? Some pieces will sell for three times what you paid. Arrange with a truck-owner for deliveries twice a week, (Mondays and Thursdays) but urge most Buyers to pick up. Be prepared to discount your prices --people who buy used furniture are looking for bargains. Don't be concerned that there is another used furniture outlet in town (or several in a city). Used furniture is becoming more and more popular. Pricing in this business, when buying or selling is a very important skill to be developed. It will take time to learn what various items should be bought and sold for. Start by visiting used furniture outlets to compare prices being asked.

SEWING/ALTERATIONS

Notice all the thrift stores that are springing up? Each one would sell more clothes if able to refer customers to a place that does alterations at a reasonable price. If you have a sewing machine, are able to "take in" or "let out" dresses, slacks, trousers, etc. visit all the thrift stores and clothing stores to acquaint them with your "alterations service." Give them a supply of your business cards to hand out ($10 for 1000 cards at Staples). Properly handled, you can build your alterations business (done from home) to point where you need to hire help. Charge reasonable prices to begin with. When you have plenty jobs to do you can raise prices.

This is a business that can be started with practically no investment. You may want to buy one or two clothing- dummies, but not necessary. This can be a very profitable business, Remember, "As you sew, so shall you reap." The Thrift stores in your area can keep you as busy as you want to be, making alterations and then pressing the garments. Ask them to put up a sign showing your prices for various alterations. Remind them they will sell more clothing if it can be altered to fit at a low price. Within a few months you probably will need to obtain additional help?

Notes on this business:

GOWN RENTALS

Some brides spend several hundreds of dollars for a wedding gown, never use it again. Offer to sell it from your home on consignment basis. Same thing with formal dresses and gowns; they are expensive, but seldom worn and in most cases don't fit any more. You can sell gowns on consignment or buy them at very low price and rent them out, just as some places rent formal evening wear to men. Because alterations often are involved, this is ideal "tie-in" business for those able to do alterations. Use simple, PVC pipe rack to hang gowns (on wheels, so can be moved to a closet or out of sight when no customers coming). How much should you charge to rent a gown for one evening? $35 to $50 is not much to pay for wearing an expensive gown on a very special occasion. It will have to be cleaned after use. Alterations should be extra, of course. And you might stock some accessory items for sale, including pre-owned, matching shoes. This can be a very profitable business with little or no competition. See the "Sales Promotion" chapter for ideas on how to build this business.

FUND RAISING BUSINESS

In every town are hundreds of civic organizations that continually need to raise money to fund their activities. There are women's clubs, garden clubs, men's clubs, political groups-- all kinds of organizations, including girl and boy scout troops, athletic clubs, churches, etc. Schools have marching bands, athletic teams, debating teams, all kinds of groups that every year need money to fund travel, outings, parties and celebrations.

These groups get their money mostly by raising funds from the sale of cookies, candy bars, by washing cars, by giving performances.

You can help these groups to raise money with "scratch cards." The members ask friends, neighbors, anyone they meet to scratch off a box on a card. Underneath it gives the amount to be donated -- from 25 cents up to (perhaps) $3. Each card will raise $25 to $50. By getting (say) 25 members to go around with a scratch card, the group can raise over $1000.

You contact the civic, social, and school groups and acquaint them with this fast and easy way to raise money. You take their order for the number of scratch cards wanted (*They don't need to pay anything in advance --they pay AFTER the cards have brought in the targeted goal of X dollars*).

Several companies manufacture scratch cards for fund raising. Find them on the Internet by typing in "scratch cards," or "Fund Raising." Some of the companies pay a commission of forty to fifty percent. Some companies include a coupon good for a movie admission or for half-off at McDonald's or Burger King. Donors don't mind scratching off an amount when they get a coupon that may be worth more than their donation.

This business can be run from home, requires little or no investment and can produce an income of several thousand dollars a year. It's a particularly good business for a housewife with social contacts and an outgoing personality.

To get started. make your connection with a scratch card supplier. Most of them supply a manual that teaches you how to get and handle orders. Essentially, you tell groups how they can quickly raise big money with scratch cards and with no up-front money. And there's no up-front money required from you. either.

You can start this business with $10 for business cards.

COMPUTER INK-CARTRIDGE SELLER

The ink cartridges for computer printers are expensive, ranging from $20 to $35 for about six ounces of ink, about $10 -$15 more for color ink. The ink containers (the cartridges) probably cost more to make than does the ink. There is money to be made buying ink in bulk and re-filling the plastic cartridges.

The way this business works is to require buyers to supply an empty cartridge which you either refill while they wait or for them to pick-up next day or you replace with same cartridge already refilled (you can buy the most popular brands of re-filled replacement cartridges and stock them). A re-filled replacement cartridge costs the consumer about half the price of a new cartridge. You could make $10 to $15 on each sale.

You also can buy new cartridges of the popular makes at wholesale and make a profit selling these when buyer doesn't have a replacement cartridge to trade-in or have refilled.

The refilling of ink cartridges requires little space, can be done in basement or garage. Look on the

Internet for suppliers of ink in bulk and refill kits, or in public library Directory of Manufacturers. Keep in mind that different makes of printers require a specific type of ink. Check to see if there already is too much competition in your area. *Warning: the high prices for ink cartridges may fade away because of growing consumer resistance to the high prices.*

Notes on this business:

HEALTH AND FITNESS BUSINESS

More and more emphasis is being placed on the importance of taking positive steps to improve one's health and fitness. You can cash in on this trend.

Contact the local YMCA or YWCA or a local church having a good-size meeting room. Ask to rent space for a fitness class to be held every day (except Sunday). Attendees will be mostly females, but more men will come Saturdays. Sessions could be one hour or two.

Get exercise (jazzercise) videos from local public library or video rental store. Study and practice the exercises until you can lead a group doing the jazzercises. Use an audiocassette to play music for the sessions (should have a pronounced beat). If shower/changing rooms available that's a plus, but not really necessary. Let the pheromones flow.

Charge as little at $4 per person per session to get started (price you charge depends upon rental cost of space). You can offer a discount for ten sessions. When you have at least 20 people showing up regularly you will be earning decent income.

It may take a month or two to attract enough participants, but if you make the sessions informal, fun, and accept that socializing is almost as important as the exercising, you could build this business into a real money-maker from referrals alone. Use of name tags is good idea, to get attendees acquainted with each other.

To build this businesses use bulletin board notices and distribute circulars, perhaps run a three-line ad in the classifieds under "Personals." Have bottled water on hand in a cooler to distribute on the "break." A few hours of your time each day can produce a good income and the enjoyment of relating to lots of people, PLUS keep you in good shape.

NOTES ON THIS BUSINESS:

MAIL ORDER

Perhaps thousands of people are running a mail order business from their home. It seems so easy; you just write a letter and enclose a product sheet and perhaps a return envelope. Then you wait for the replies to come pouring in, each one containing a check. Sorry, it ain't that easy. While it takes only a few hundred dollars to get into mail order business, you can go broke sending out letters or brochures because the response rate may be only one or two percent (average) - often not enough to cover costs of mailing never mind costs of product.

There are big fat books available on how to be successful in the mail order business. Let's see if we can boil them down to essentials: (1) You should be a competent writer (2) You need to have an inherent ability to be persuasive, (3) You need a product that cannot be purchased for less money at Wal-Mart, Walgreen's, K-Mart, or other low-price outlets and (4) that product has to have an attractive selling price even if it is three or four times your cost, (5) You must have a good mailing list consisting of people or companies which are first-class prospects for what you are selling (buying or compiling that list can be very expensive), (6) You need an appealing product that is easily shipped at low cost, (7) does not require a large inventory because you easily can replace the inventory or the product will be shipped to customers by manufacturers or distributors you buy from.

The most profitable, easily handled item to sell is *information,* either printed on paper, on an audio or videocassette or on a CD or DVD. The information has to be valuable or entertaining to the people you reach.

The mail order business, consisting of letters, brochures, catalogs, etc., is fast giving way to selling on the Internet. There you can reach millions of people without the nuisance of printing, mailing, buying stamps, envelopes, etc., etc. In a few years there will less than half the catalog mailers existing today. Many are failing now-- out of date because of today's fast growing information systems on Internet.

But, hey, don't let me discourage you. With the right product, good persuasive copy in letters or small ads, some people are racking up big incomes. Mostly they are pro's who have learned from trial and error - a costly process. Approach this business with caution.

MASSAGE THERAPIST

Don't let the title lead you to think you need to be a professional. What you can offer without pro training is a "Relaxation Massage." All you need is a folding massage table (or any portable table with a cushion),a couple of sheets, and some body oil.

The massage business is booming as more people learn to enjoy the feeling of peace and relaxation that comes from someone massaging their body. Some executives today have a masseuse (female) or a masseur (male) come in during office hours to relieve the tension and stress involved in their job. But mostly it involves giving the massage in someone's apartment or home, or at a Health Fair, a day-cruise ship concession, local carnival, etc.

Look into licensing requirements, if any. It is illegal to make therapeutic claims. Simply state that you give "Relaxation Massages". All you need do is rub the muscles at the base of the neck, the shoulders, the upper back muscles, and the muscles around the hips and small of the back and legs.. You could bring a small cassette player and play a tape of music especially recorded for relaxation. Or you could give slow, low, voice commands to "Relax," or "Let go" while you are gently rubbing the client's back(a client is not "a patient").

It would be a mistake to keep up a stream of chatter--the client wants to relax, not listen to your banter or jokes. Let clients lead the talking. Keep quiet otherwise.

As stated, you need not be a pro. However, there are schools that teach massage techniques in a 90-days-or less course.

You probably can find a book or video on massage techniques at public library. Get some practice by massaging your spouse or a friend. Fees range from $25 to $100 per half-hour, depending on where done. You will need to be able to massage those of the opposite sex without being "turned on" sexually. Otherwise there could be trouble. Not a safe business for the recently married. Some massage parlors are sexually-oriented, running the risk of jail-time. There's a trade magazine: " *Massage Therapy Journal"* 820 Davis St. Evanston. Illinois.

*(*See our "Recommended Books" section).

MODEL AGENCY

If you live in a city having (say) over 50,000 population the chances are good that you can make a decent income in your spare time by running an agency that supplies models for TV commercials, for local magazines, fashion shows, store openings, business shows , public functions,

You will need to sign up attractive children and women and men of all ages who are able to take some time away from school or from their job to pose for photo "shoots."

A classified ad inviting submission of two photos (face and full length) will produce many applicants. You will need to interview those you select and to sign them to a modeling contract (by parents for children). The hourly rate for local models varies from $75 to $100 of which you would get 15 to 25 percent. (*See sample modeling contracts at public library reference section*)

Your next task will be to get jobs for the models. For this purpose you could run a continuous one column by one inch display ad "Available, Models of all ages - For TV commercials and Public Functions." It is important to visit all ad agencies in your area, TV stations, local magazines, major department stores and those high-end clothing retailers continually using news- paper advertising. Bring with you a circular and a scrapbook containing some photos of your models. (It is useful to have a connection with a professional photog who has a studio) When ready, you could have a well-publicized party for models, media, etc. to get off to a noticed start-up with prospective clients.

It's wise to carry a supply of business cards so you can give one to an attractive woman or man you believe is photogenic. However, if your intentions are not honorable you could be reported to police for "soliciting," which may lead to adverse newspaper stories. Many individuals now are in prison for using "Want to be a model" scam to lure young people into paying fees or into illegal activities, If you get a bad reputation you may as well fold the business -- TV stations, magazines, and other potential clients will not want to be associated with you and you will be made to feel unwelcome in your neighborhood, community, and among acquaintances.

License requirements vary with each State and city. Your first step will be to determine what these requirements are. License applications may want details of any past difficulties with the law.

Run properly, this can be an interesting and profitable part- time business that can be run from home. Applicants and clients can be met in a hotel lobby or at an upscale restaurant. It is important to create a professional image. Dress for the part.

SINGLES PARTY GIVER

Do you like to party? Most people do, especially if they can meet interesting people and perhaps a lover. Singles are great party-goers. You can rent a meeting room that will hold up to 100 Singles in an easy-to- find hotel or motel or even a progressive-minded church. Use a name that indicates it is a club, like "Beautiful Singles" Register the club name at Occupation License bureau. Run an ad and (better) get a story in local newspaper. At the party you should have soft, taped music and perhaps 10 chairs and NO tables except registration table. People should sign in, giving their name and telephone number (so they become "Members") The objective is to have attendees stand and move around the room meeting people. Many will pair off for dancing (There should be much slow dancing, little rock and roll) Each person should get a sticky label with their first name printed in large block letters plus a number.

Wine (white and "blush") can be served (in plastic cups from gallon bottles), not hard liquor.(If not a registered club you would need a liquor license). Give three tickets for drinks -different color for males. Stop excessive drinking by anyone. Take steps to limit everyone to three drinks.

Dress can be casual. but no shorts permitted (as stated in your ad and in newspaper story)

The parties could be scheduled Friday or Saturday nite from 8 P.M. to 11 P.M. In some areas you could run it both nights every week. You could run similar parties in adjacent towns?   You could give door prizes (hence the number on name label) and announce any special function you are running, such as Sunday beach get-together or day or evening cruise. any kind of group activity you organize.

Admission to the party could be $6.50 with wine included. (maximum three drinks). You do not want anyone to get drunk.

You can clear several hundred dollars per party if you run it right -- making it fun but not rowdy (A good idea is to have two "bouncers" who politely, but firmly ask anyone causing trouble to leave). If parties are rowdy they will fail.   Believe it, this kind of party attracted over 300 Singles every week for many years in an area of several close-by towns in Connecticut -- and the parties were held in a church

150

hall over those years. It was good fun for all, run by volunteers. The church got a small rental fee.

PET CEMETERY

Pet burials can become a big business - and so can pet cremations. What would YOU do if YOUR dog or cat died? Look in the Yellow Pages to see if there are any competitors offering pet burials. Most likely there aren't.   Next thing to do is check on what zoning laws will permit?

You then could seek an outlying acre or so, properly zoned, which you can buy or lease with a few hundred dollars down (subject to your getting necessary permits). You then may need to rent trench digging equipment (depends on how difficult it is to dig a deep hole in the soil?-- a pick and shovel may do?). You also will need a nice entrance and a parking area. A motion detector can set off an alarm to scare off intruders seeking to bury pet themselves at night.

Make an arrangement with a monument company to refer your customers (on a commission basis) in case some people don't want the standard grave marker you should supply (one easy to attach pre-cut letters on and weather proof)). Prepare a burial speech so you or pet owner can say a standard farewell (with the pet's name added). Some of your customers may need a consoling session with a sympathetic person you recommend (on commission basis). Keep in mind that most people truly love their pet. Its loss can be an emotional trauma. You should conduct yourself accordingly - dignity and sympathy are called for. It's a solemn funeral business. You may want to sell small, wood caskets you purchase elsewhere or a plastic box with a lid , perhaps covered with cloth?

This can become a high income business. Look up suppliers for pet cemeteries in a reference book at the library. You may need a vehicle and the stamina to transport dead animals, but most people will bring the deceased pet to you. Look into required licenses in your city and/or state - if any?

Notes on this business:

SWIMMING POOL SERVICES

This is a nice business for individuals who like working outdoors, but it is limited to certain geographical areas --like Florida, California, and the Deep South. In other areas there may be too few swimming pools to produce a decent income every month? It can be entered with very little cash.

You'll need a skimmer-net on a long pole, some brushes on a pole, some cleansers, some chemicals (like chlorine, etc.) and an acid-alkaline pH measurement device (minimum requirements).

But you do need to know about the chemicals used to keep swimming pools free of algae, slime, and pathogenic organisms that cause illness. Fortunately there are many books and booklets on how to care for swimming pools. Also, the store where you buy professional pool equipment and needed chemicals often will give you good practical advice. As anyone who has owned a swimming pool knows, they require lots of attention. Mostly, pool cleaning and maintenance is done on a contract basis --perhaps twice a month, but often, once a week.

One information source is *Service Industry Publications,* P.O. Box 2909, Torrance, California 90509. Another is *Taylor Technologies, Inc. Sparks, Maryland 21152* (They have free booklets on pool and spa water chemistry). Your public library also is a likely source of information.

This is a great business for those who like to work outdoors and to meet people who lounge around the swimming pool. A great many women do pool cleaning. As for prices for this service, it varies so much geographically that any estimate will be misleading. Your best bet is to call persons in this business and find out what they are charging. You also can find out by talking to people who own a swimming pool and asking what they are paying for pool maintenance. Again, it is very important to know how to control the pH balance and how to use safe, bacteria-control chemicals. Make sure you know what you are doing. Health is involved.

Customers will be not only private pool owners, but also condominiums, hotels, motels, and spas. You also could sell various chemicals, pool toys, and child-alert signals that sound an alarm when a child falls into an unwatched pool (the wave rocks the unit, resulting in an electrical contact). You could run this business in warm months, also run one where it is warm in the winter -- a good life. *Check yellow pages to see how much competition there is, but "there is always room for one more."*

TRACING UNCLAIMED MONEY

Over $2 billions are lying in U.S. bank vaults, unclaimed, and because of upheavals in Europe since 1935 there is even more unclaimed money in European banks, on deposit by those who had to flee their country in order to survive and who may never have been heard from again. Their relatives may be the beneficiaries. This is particularly the case with Jews, but they usually have Jewish organizations doing the searching. Every State requires banks to file reports on deposits unclaimed for a specified number of years. Banks often advertise to locate depositors and heirs, but most of money is never claimed.

You can offer to help individuals (the general public) find out if there is money in the bank which they or a family member forgot about or which, unknowingly, was left to them by relatives with no Will filed with the courts.

It often takes very little time to search the records using a computer. You can offer to make a computer search for a few dollars, OR at no charge unless money is found, in which case you could ask for 25 to 50 percent of the recovered amount.

You also can use a computer to determine the value of old stocks and bonds found in the attic or other places.

While the corporation which issued the stock or bonds may no longer be in business, its assets and liabilities may have been acquired by a corporation whose shares now are actively trading and thus is still liable for the value of the old shares. Old stock and bonds can be valuable for other reasons, some too complicated for this book.

Anyone going into this business should have lots of computer-smarts and be aware there are many pro's and firms already in this business, most of whom are making big bucks. However, most people don't know about these kinds of services. Run small classified ad under "Personals."   Easily run this biz in spare time if you have computer-smarts.

USED COMPUTERS EXCHANGE

Many computer owners and businesses will upgrade their computer(s) every few years, especially if the computers are on an expiring lease. Usually they then can purchase their computer(s) at a low price, get a higher price by selling the computer(s) themselves. Also, because computers constantly are being improved, it often makes sense to sell one's present computer, even though it is in top operating condition, in order to get more speed, bigger hard drive, larger screen.

Many individuals buying their first computer will be interested in getting started with a used computer that cost only $150 to $250, including the monitor and printer.

For these and other good reasons you can make money by selling used computers, monitors, printers, and other related items from your home, your garage, or a rented storage space. Get the computers on consignment and ask (say) a 20 percent commission on the selling price. When you know what the prices should be, you often will be able to buy used computers outright at low prices for resale.

To promote your business distribute circulars to all the large companies in your area advising that you can get a good price for their used computers. Then run a small classified ad under "Computers For Sale" heading in local news- paper. Also, visit all the places selling new computers and acquaint them with your "used" business. It can help them make sales of new PC's, (but some also sell used models).

It is important that those consigning a computer to you for sale will guarantee the computer is in good working condition. Do not pay them for 3 days after their computer has been sold. However, you should be able to plug in the computers and demo their working condition. Same with printers. You should know how to operate a computer, but if you don't you soon will learn simple demo procedures.

All it takes to get started in this business is $25 worth of circulars. a small classified ad, a selling space, and some hustle. You can run this business in spare time - evenings and week-ends. Start by checking amount of competition. Don't let a few competitors scare you off. Research them.

WINDOW CLEANING SERVICE

This isn't a glamorous business, but it can produce an income of $30,000 a year in many areas. To start with you could do mostly retail stores where you don't need to use a ladder (a box 6 to 8 inches high could be very useful for short people as will an extension handle).

The equipment needed is not expensive. You need a professional grade squeegee (if you use household-type you will spend time re-doing your work), and you need to use the best cleaning liquids, bought wholesale from a janitorial supply company. Many window-cleaners use a chamois (shammy) cloth to give windows a polished look.

Most home cleaning services don't do window cleaning. Contact them for leads. You can clean windows in homes and offices and make $20 an hour- - more if you need to use a step ladder or scaffold (Don't use one if you get dizzy at heights).

This is a business for males or females. Get customers by having a circular printed (1000 for about $25), distribute them to homes in upper income areas and hand them out to retail stores all over town.

If you become very busy, hire others and focus on getting more customers. Be sure to contact property management firms. They often handle condos and office buildings and will be the contracting entity. Most work will be done on a contract basis, like once a week for retail stores and twice a month for offices

(See reference books at public library for samples of applicable contracts. Ask librarian for help, if needed).

Notes on this business:

WORKSHEET FOR A BUSINESS OF INTEREST

If any of the businesses described are of interest to you, take a few moments to answer some questions that will help you decide whether you should give it further consideration? Once again, it almost always is a mistake to go into a business you won't enjoy or which calls for skills you do not have and are not interested in acquiring.

	Yes	No
Does the type of work involved in this business really appeal to you?	( )	( )
Do you have the personal qualities needed to make a success of this particular business?	( )	( )
Will this business require working early in the morning or late at night. If so, is this acceptable	( )	( )
Are there now a great many competitors ? (See Yellow Pages in phone book).	( )	( )

If this business requires equipment
or tools, can you afford to spend
the money to get them?   ( )   ( )

If this business requires leasing
space can you afford to pay rent
for many months w/o income?   ( )   ( )

Do you have enough money to go
into this business without putting
yourself or others at serious risk?   ( )   ( )

Can you, if necessary, go without
income from this business for
(say) three to six months?   ( )   ( )

Based upon a rough estimate of
how much you can earn from this
business, is that amount satisfactory?   ( )   ( )

Is this a business you will be ashamed
to let your friends or others know
you are in ?   ( )   ( )

Will this business enable you
to put into play the special skills
or talents you have ?   ( )   ( )
Are you willing to put in the
time and effort that may be
required to become really good
at this business?   ( )   ( )

*It is advisable to think about this business for a
couple of days and to talk about it with those involved
or whose judgment you respect before taking
actions. Keep in mind that it is easier for friends to
discourage you and thus have no responsibility for the
outcome, than it is to encourage you and take some
blame if the business doesn't work out. Also, every
business, without exception, has its drawbacks. If
the drawbacks were focused on, nobody would go
into business -- or own a dog.*

A SEPARATE WORD ABOUT COMPUTER-BASED BUSINESSES

Businesses based upon a computer and the Internet are sprouting up overnight like mushrooms. There are, without exaggeration, more than 100 businesses you could go into if you are computer literate. And everyone of them can be operated from home, whether that home is in Montana, the Virgin Isles, or San Francisco. When you are connected to the Internet you are connected to millions of computers around the world - and people who own computers can be good prospects for whatever you are selling. It is likely that within five years millions more people will have bought a computer, adding to the more than 250 millions around the world who already own one.

Online Retailing

Anything sold in a store can be sold on the Internet. It is like retailing using a catalog, except you don't have printing and mailing costs. Prospects visit your site (page), select the item(s) they want, pay electronically (there are many money collecting services which will accept credit cards then send the money to your bank account) You then have the item(s) shipped by the manufacturers or wholesalers to the buyers. You can do it all sitting at home in your underwear.

Sounds easy, doesn't it? It isn't! The problem is how to get people to visit your site. There are mega-million sites on the Internet. You could spend a fortune trying to get traffic to your site - without much success. One way to get visitors to your site is to rent a virtual store in an Internet "Shopping Mall." The owners of the Mall spend time and money attracting visitors to their Mall and to the virtual stores in the Mall --such as yours.   There are hundreds of such Malls. Some succeed in attracting shoppers, others fail at it. The "rent" could be wasted money. If you can find a really good and unique product at the right price, it's worth a try. Get figures on how much traffic goes to "Mall," before signing up.

Selling "Information"

Our times have been called "The Information Age." Useful and timely information is worth money -- like a tip on the stockmarket. Right now there are thousands of databases (virtual files) containing valuable information. You can access these and get information to sell to people and companies who will turn that information into a profit. Every day someone or some company comes up with new "software" (tools) to obtain information faster, more reliably, more usefully. No question about it - skill on a computer can be translated into big money - as employee or entrepreneur. Some examples of the businesses you can go into with a computer:

Bankruptcy Advice (including needed forms)
Genealogy Consultant (Help people trace their ancestry)
Finding People (computer makes it simple)
Mortgage Loan Broker (You just take applications, sell them to mortgage firms.

Credit Card Advisor (Where to get lowest interest, etc.)

Online Dating Service   (Introduce men and women for a fee)

Immigration Consultant (Advise those seeking citizenship)

Employment Agency (Find job openings for people based upon their resume)

Incorporation Services   It just takes simple forms in most States. You can offer these forms and help incorporate

100 more businesses could be listed which require little more than computer expertise. If you are not good on the computer, pay someone to teach you. If you are really good on the computer teach others for a fee of $30 to $45 per hour. Look in our "Best Books Index for the best book to buy on various computer businesses and how to run them. Being computer-literate is becoming a requirement in our society. If you don't have a computer it's like not having a telephone, and not being able to use a computer is almost like not having a driver's license.

Your local library undoubtedly has computers and may offer computer classes for beginners. People age75 and up are becoming computer-literate. It's becoming easier and easier to operate a computer. Kids age 6 can do it! But, no question about it, the companies that manufacture operating systems (like "Windows") have been too slow in simplifying the basics of computer operation. (Are you listening, Microsoft and Apple?)

WHAT FORM OF BUSINESS SHOULD YOU USE?

There are three main types of business ownership: The sole proprietor, the partnership, the corporation. Usually, the one-person business operates as a proprietorship. But this is not necessarily the best form for a one-person business. If there are risks of being sued over your products or services (for example, if your home-made food products could make someone ill) then you may want to use the corporate form of doing business because it ordinarily limits liability to the value of the assets used in the business.

The sole proprietorship is the simplest form of business ownership. If you use your own name, such as "John Smith -Painting" you may not need an occupational license. Most businesses, however, do need an occupational license (cost $10 to $50), especially if using a made-up name (like "Superior Landscaping Company") Check with the Town Clerk or County Clerk's office about occupational license requirements.

The sole proprietorship involves the least amount of government red-tape. Your business income will be taxed just like personal income. The profits and losses are all yours when you fill out your income tax form (except that if you do not make a profit for three years in a row the government may claim you are not in business to make a profit but merely to take tax benefits available to business owners). Disadvantages of a sole proprietorship are (1) full financial responsibility in legal actions, (2) it suggests "small time" operation, (3) personal liability for loans and unpaid bills incurred by the business.

The partnership divides responsibility and work duties, lessens the personal Investment requirement. Can be good if each partner contributes different skills and abilities. The partners share profit and losses, report them on their individual tax return. However, partnerships, even between good friends or relatives often lead to disputes and legal actions. Finding the right partner involves more careful analysis than hiring a manager or employee. Proceed cautiously.

You should enjoy being in business. Your partner could drive you up the wall.

The corporation involves issuing stock to owners and investors. It is far easier to incorporate a business than most people realize. In most States you do not need a lawyer; you simply fill out forms costing $50 to $100 to file (obtain forms from State capitol). However, you will need a corporate record book, perhaps a corporate seal, and other required items. These usually can be obtained at an office supply store or at a corporate-supplies firm located in the State capitol area. Some law firms specialize in corporation formation and many offer a complete package for about $100 to $125.

The best part of having a corporation are the tax benefits involved, the limited liability, the ability to sell stock to raise money, plus many benefits you can give yourself (and there a great many, including a pension plan, medical insurance, etc.) It is even possible to "go public" without registration of the new stock issue by following SEC regulations.

Most States require payment of an annual fee to continue a corporation. Look into this fee before deciding to incorporate. The fees can be hefty and the reporting requirements a nuisance. Visit a public library for corporate rules in your State. There are various types of corporations you can use: ""S" corporation," "Limited Liability", others. Look into these forms before deciding which form is best for your purposes.

SELECT A USEFUL NAME FOR YOUR BUSINESS

It should be distinctive, easy to remember, indicative of what your business does. For example, instead of "Ajax Company" you will gain an advantage by indicating what the company does, such as "Ajax Publishing Company. The shorter the name the less cost involved when advertising in classified pages and the easier it is to remember. Would you use "Ajax Publishing, Printing & Binding Company?" Assuredly not. And if you are going to have a website, a short name easily can be used for your URL and for email. It is a good idea to search out your intended business name to make sure it is not already being used by someone else. Before you order stationery and business cards check the Yellow Pages, computer search engines, and the business names already registered with the city or county clerk or at the State capitol. You can use a name not registered in your State.

RECORD KEEPING - A NECESSARY NUISANCE

Most individuals going into business hate the necessity for keeping accurate records of every transaction, perhaps for as long as three years, and keeping track of all expenses and sources of income, plus retaining receipts and invoices for everything bought or sold.

You can simplify record keeping to some extent by having a separate bank account for your business, paying every bill by check --even for one or two dollars and depositing all income rather than just stuffing some of it into your wallet.

With good records, however, you will be able to simplify your tax returns, get bank loans easier, and be able to calculate your profits and losses and make adjustments to purchase and sale prices. If you hate working with figures, hire a part-time bookkeeper or talk your spouse into doing the record keeping (if you want to get divorced).

But don't settle for sloppy record keeping. It will come back to make your business life miserable-- especially on April 15th.

OBTAINING AN EIN

Regardless of the form of business you chose it is a good idea to get an Employers Identification Number (EIN) from the federal government. An EIN identifies your business for federal tax purposes and MUST be obtained if you pay an employee, even if that employee is yourself only. From your wages your should deduct and remit Social Security taxes, Unemployment deductions, and then file estimated tax forms (If employed by another company and deductions are taken from your wages, you may NOT have to file estimated taxes). Because of the reporting requirements, some business owners do not pay themselves a regular wage, but instead withdraw money as a loan from the company. In any case, a record must be kept of the money paid to you by the business, either as salary, as profits, or as a loan, and reported as income when filing a tax return (To get an EIN use form SS-4)

COLLECTING SALES TAXES

If you are selling something subject to sales taxes you MUST obtain a permit from your State to collect the sales taxes and remit the taxes as scheduled. Or, in some States you can simply pay the sales taxes yourself on all your sales. Typical of bureaucratic arrogance, some States make you pay a fee in order to collect sales taxes for them.

TAX ADVANTAGES IN YOUR OWN BUSINESS

The average wage earner pays federal and State income taxes, local real estate taxes, sales taxes, taxes on telephone usage, cable TV, on movie admissions, airline travel, gasoline, and on many other goods and services-- all adding up to roughly fifty percent of income. It reminds one of the old joke "My employer wants me to work only half a day. He doesn't care what I do in the other twelve hours."

With your own business you can qualify for a great many tax deductions. For example, if you use your vehicle (say) fifty percent for business purposes in an attempt to make a profit and fifty percent for personal use, you can deduct 50 percent of all the costs associated with the purchase and operation of that vehicle, including depreciation, insurance. tolls, license fees, gasoline, etc. these deductions can save you hundred of dollars you otherwise would pay to the government in taxes.

179

With a business you can claim as a deduction a share of your telephone bill, can depreciate any office equipment or furniture, and even deduct the cost of medical insurance. You can even claim a deduction for business use of your home (However this deduction is so often challenged by the IRS it may not be worth claiming).

You can also claim a deduction for business lunches, dinners, and entertaining. On this subject please understand that in order to justify such deductions you MUST be able to produce evidence for them. That means you have to save all receipts, be able to document all expenditures, keep a record of all expenses, vehicle mileage, even toll receipts. This is one reason why most people in business use a separate credit card for business expenditures. The monthly credit card statements provide a written record, especially for business travel (You can bring your wife on business trips and deduct her costs if you introduce her to prospects, clients or associates). This enables you to claim tax deductions for vacations if the vacations clearly have a business purpose attached to them.

Hire Your Wife (And Children)

If your spouse and/or children help with the business you can pay them a salary and deduct their pay as a business expense. Salaries paid to children are non-taxable (up to a specified limit). However, reports are required that entail lots of paper work, but it could be worth the trouble. Keep in mind that if you report a loss three years in a row the government may disallow all business deductions in the fourth year if you do not show a profit.

Note: What is being said here about tax deductions is not offered as expert advice. Tax rules change almost every year. You should buy the latest tax-help book -- the soft-cover kind people buy around income tax time for $5 to $10.

Tax-deferred Retirement Fund

The IRS permits the owner of a business to put a portion of earnings into a pension funds, even if an employer already gives you a pension account.

There are many other tax advantages in owning a business. We can't cover them all here, are merely showing some tax advantages in being a business owner. No doubt about it - a business can be the best tax shelter one can have. Properly handled a business can escape all taxes on income. Many giant corporations with profits in the hundreds of millions of dollars have paid no taxes on those profits whatsoever.

TOOLS TO HELP YOU MAKE SALES

Accepting Credit Cards

A large percentage of sales to consumers today involve the use of a credit card. In order for you to accept them you will need a "Merchant's Account." This involves being tied in by telephone line to a credit card processor. The cost of needed equipment is about $1500, a hefty sum. And you will have to pay the credit card processing firm 2 to 3 percent of the sales amount as a handling fee To spend this much money is justified only if your sales will be boosted significantly by accepting credit cards. An alternative is available to those with a computer: there are several firms on the Internet that will accept credit card charges on your behalf and credit the amount to your bank account. They want up to 10 percent of the sales amount as a fee. Not all of these credit card- accepting firms are trustworthy. Choose carefully and monitor your statements closely. "Mistakes" are common.

Toll Free Phone Number

If your business is such that many of your customers or prospects must pay a toll call to reach you, it may be advisable to get a toll-free number from the phone company. This is not expensive, can be installed on your single line and set up with a different ring than your regular ring signal. You even can get a toll-free number that spells out your business name "1-800-REPAIRS", for example. Going to bed at night you can turn off the ringer on the phone. Alternatively, if you plan to get lots of phone calls you can use an answering service for about $20 a month. If you are going to be making a great many long-distance phone calls, it may be economical to get a flat rate for an unlimited amount of long distance phone calls (about $50 a month).

Direct Mail

Mailings are expensive at present first-class rate of 37 cents per letter. Post cards might do the job just as well for 23 cents per card. If you are going to do frequent mailings you should look into getting a bulk-mail permit which enables you to mail 200 pieces of mail at a time for a reduced rate (Your Post Office will give you details and rates). However, bulk mailings can be more trouble than they are worth, with the post office often requiring the mailing pieces to be sorted and bundled by zip code.

Bulk Emailings

With a computer, you can send tens of thousands of email letters in less than a half hour - with no postage cost! You can buy software that enables you to do bulk emailings or you use services of an emailing firm at less cost than stamps. However, most bulk emailings are seen as "spam," and spamming is against the law. One has to be very careful about emails, sending only to those who have given their permission to receive emails (opt-in's). Despite the laws many bulk- email firms exist. They can supply email addresses of millions of computer owners around the world and software that enables you to collect email addresses off the Internet and send out (say) 500,000 emails in a couple of hours. It's a great marketing tool. How long it will remain legal is uncertain. Still, you can send "spam" type emails to the millions of prospects in other countries which do not have spam-laws.

Telephone Answering Machine

If you don't already have one you are missing important phone calls. You need one for your business. How do you keep your business calls separate from your personal calls? --Simple! Get an answering machine with two or more "Mail" (message) boxes. Then, just like the big corporations you ask the caller to select the extension wanted - "personal" or "business." Cost is as low as $49,-- a little more money and you can get one with three or more message-boxes.

Government Assistance

The federal government wants to assist small business formation and so, offers financing and tons of information about starting and running a small business. The Small Business Administration offers many services. Write to them (see Gov't Resources page) and ask for catalog of publications and how to qualify for a loan. One booklet you might start with is "Marketing For Small Business." Send $1 to *SBA Publications, P.O. Box 130, Denver, CO 80201.*

(See "Sales Promotion" pages for more ideas)

SALES PROMOTION IDEAS

The primary objective of every business, from General Motors to Aunt Millie's Yarn Shoppe, is to attract enough customers to pay all expenses and make a profit.

The usual way to get customers is to advertise. However, a small business can go broke by spending too much on advertising. It often does NOT pay to advertise, especially if yours is a small business and you don't have much capital. When advertising it is advisable to avoid so called "Goodwill" advertising, in which you just mention the name of your store or business and do not make an attractive offer. An "attractive" offer is one that <u>attracts</u> people, makes sales. A basic rule in advertising is "Give people a reason for coming to you."

There are several low-cost ways to promote sales without spending a lot of money. Here are a few of them:

Circulars

You can get 1000 circulars printed for about $25. Distribute them to your primary customers. If you want to reach the general public, place a circular under the windshield wiper of vehicles (or give some high school kid a few dollars to do it.) The best places are shopping centers, movie theatres, anywhere a large number of vehicles are parked. If you want to reach home owners, the circulars should be distributed house to house. If you want to reach retail stores, -- well, you get the idea -- distribute your circulars to your best prospects. More important, word your circular so it will attract interest. Giving a discount or embedding a coupon is a good idea, but have it expire in a week or two. You want action.

Classified Ads

These can produce good results for you, but need to be well written to attract customers in only a few lines. Write out what you want to say in your ad, then spend time trying to say the same thing in fewer words. Your objective should be to write a good ad in just three or four lines. Run it for about a week to see if it produces results. Get the "Contract Rate" in which you agree to use a specified number of lines a year (Don't worry about not using that many. If you don't, most newspapers will not give you a hard time.)

If the ad doesn't get good results, change it after a trial. Ask the Classified Ad people at the newspaper to help word your ad, if not confident of your own ability.   The right classification is very important. Compare classified cost with cost of one column, one inch display ad.

"Take One" Displays

You undoubtedly have seen these little boxes containing folders or booklets with the words "Take One" printed on the display unit.   (Credit card companies use them extensively.) You can buy clear plastic displays at Staples or Office Depot for about $2 each. Put a gummed label on the front of them that says "FREE - TAKE ONE" then place these little display units in stores having heavy traffic -- like dry cleaners, liquor stores, etc. -- giving the owner some kind of commission on the sales made from his store. Start with about 35 booklets or circulars (folded to envelope size) in each display unit, then check on their supply every few days. In smaller towns more store owners will let you put your display unit on the counter without compensation. These "Take One" displays can reach a lot of people for a small investment.

Publicity

Getting an article about your business in the local newspaper is the lowest cost way to attract customers, and perhaps the most powerful. Find out who the Business Reporter is and send him/her a story about your new business. Better yet, telephone that reporter and urge him/her to visit you for the "inside" story. Whenever you have an "angle" (an interesting occurrence) send the reporter a story about it. If possible and appropriate enclose a photo whenever a photo will enliven the story. You also can get a mention on local radio and TV stations if you can make the story newsworthy.

Meetings

If you have a product or service that will be of interest to a group of people (for example an exciting new product or program that can be sold to a group) you could rent meeting space at the YMCA or a church, or any low cost meeting space. You will need to run a display ad to announce the meeting or use circulars or telephone likely prospects to urge them to attend, perhaps offering donuts and coffee for a morning meeting or lunch for a mid-morning meeting, or a door prize for an evening meeting. For example, at a meeting your could sell health foods, or a financial program, or even form a buying co-op to save money on the house painting your company does, or on storm shutters, etc. In short, if you can attract people to a meeting at low cost, use such meeting or "seminars" to get business. It's a powerful way to sell.

Direct Mail

With postage now so costly it can be expensive to send a letter to a great many prospects.

But a letter can be very effective in winning customers. Think about using postcards made from cutting white card-stock (8 1/2 x 11) into four pieces (after message has been typed on it and photocopies made).The postage for postcards is about half that for a letter and a great deal can be said on a postcard. The important thing is to target the recipients. It is a waste of money for example to send a mailing piece about house painting to people living in an apartment. In some areas you can buy a mailing list of names and addresses of people you want to reach - -like owners of boats or mobile homes-- and obtain other lists of specific prospects, from your Tax Assessors Office.

"Word of Mouth"

In smaller towns and cities where most people know each other it is very important to acquire a reputation for fair dealing, for good service, for being pleasant to deal with, for handling customer complaints fairly -- even bending over backwards to keep customers happy. In large cities this may not be as important as maximizing your profit from each customer. But in either case word-of-mouth advertising can be important, especially if large-size purchases are involved, such as vehicles or furniture. Good public relations can bring in the additional sales needed to make an average-sales day a really profitable-sales day. If fundamentally you dislike people in general but still want to go into a people-oriented business, you had better hire someone who has a pleasant personality and an easy smile to deal with prospects and customers.

Bulletin Boards

A low cost way to get business is to put a notice on public bulletin boards that can be found in supermarkets, laundromats, in other stores and places, including church bulletin boards and those found in condominium clubhouses and housing development offices. Don't just put up a business card. Put up a notice that gives people a reason to contact you. Incidentally, it's a good idea to hand out business cards everywhere you go and to everyone you meet (You can buy 1000 business cards at Staples for just $10 in a standard format). Bulletin boards can be very productive. It pays to search them out and put up a notice that gets noticed.

Local Internet Advertising

In many towns and cities there are Internet Service Providers (ISP's) which create websites for local businesses and so, provide a local advertising service for them on the Internet. You may want to have a website for your business? It is not expensive to maintain (about $10 to $12 a month). Your pages can be designed by the ISP or by a local high school or college student for a few dollars. Frankly, with the millions of pages on the Internet you can't expect much of a response unless you become part of an online "virtual mall" which spends money to create traffic to its site. You can have a "virtual store" in a virtual mall, with orders taken automatically, have the products shipped by the distributor or manufacturer. However, without a constant stream of visitors to your site (not easy to accomplish) being "on the

Internet" can be a waste of money, particularly if your customer base is mostly local.

Yellow Pages

Advertising in the Yellow Pages of the local directory can be an excellent source of customers. It's expensive, however. and you have to sign a yearly contract. Best to wait a couple of years until your business is well established and you have a lease on your location. If you do get to advertise in the Yellow Pages select the one most popular in your area when you can afford the high monthly bill. Your ad should stand out from competitive ads. The salesman contacting you should provide lots of help. But, go slow on a Yellow Pages ad.

Couponing

Everything said about advertising in the Yellow Pages applies to participating in bulk-coupon mailings offered by advertising firms. Before you do participate, call up a few of the advertisers using coupon mailings and ask about the results they obtained. You most likely will get mixed opinions, with some saying coupon mailings are a waste of money. They mostly are good for frequently purchased items, such as toiletries and grocery items. People are not likely to respond, for example, to a coupon offering a few dollars off on a vehicle or furniture or a house painting job. Investigate first!

Magnetic Sign On Car

You can get two signs made that stick to your car or truck's doors and are easily removed when using the vehicle socially. Again, don't just put your name and address on the sign, give viewers a reason for calling you, like "Best carpentry in town." or some other slogan that gives an incentive to phone you.

Mail Inserts

Try to find companies that send out lots of bills every month, such as MD's, dentists, rental firms, etc. Arrange to have a small, printed insert placed in their envelopes, perhaps paying a commission to mail on sales that result. Companies will do it on order to offset postage costs, which you might offer to share instead of paying a commission.

Door Hangers

This is an old, time-tested way of making sales. If there are a great many apartment houses or condominiums in your trading area, door hangers can quickly produce sales for you (not a good idea for single-family homes -- too time consuming). The cardboard doorhangers should contain an attractive offer with a cut-off date, so quick responses are obtained. Cost is about $75 per 1000, not cheap because of the die-cutting for the curved hangar that goes on the door knob.

Well, those a just a few ways to build your business. Keep looking for new ideas-- inexpensive ways to reach the public other than placing ads in the newspaper. Your business is not likely to be successful if you sit around waiting for people to come through the door on their own. (Unless you have the only pizza place in town). In most cases, every business will have competitors-*or soon will have if successful. Enjoy being in business for yourself, but face the reality that to make your business grow and produce a good income you are going to have to work at it, probably harder than when you were working for someone else. You will have to overcome any tendency to take things easy because you are your own boss. And it's a good idea to discourage friends from hanging around several hours a day just "shooting the breeze." If you can't do hard, physical work, focus on getting customers then hire others to do the work. That's the basis of corporate success --making money on people's labor. In any case, use promotional ideas to get business --don't just hope for it.*

SOME BUSINESS RESOURCES

(for information)

American Home Business Assn
4505 S. Wachach Blvd
Salt Lake City, Utah 84124
(800) 664-2422

Nat'l Assn for Self-Employed
P.O. Box 612067
Dallas, Texas 75261
(800) 232-NASE
www.nase.org

Direct Marketing Assn
1120 Avenue of Americas
New York. NY 10036
(212) 768-7277

American Assn of Home-Based Biz's
P.O. Box 10023
Rockville, MD 20849
www.aahbb.org

American Small Businesses Assn

8773 II Route 75E

Rock City, IL 61070

(800) 942-2722

Home Business Institute

P.O. Box 480215

Delray Beach, FL 33448

561-865-0865

National Small Business United

1152 15th Street NW

Washington, DC 20005

(202) 293-8850

www.nsbu.org

Note: Almost all these organizations can be contacted by email. Many offer low cost health insurance to members.

SOME SOURCES OF INFORMATION
USEFUL TO SMALL-BUSINESS OWNERS

<u>Some Government Sources</u>

Small Business Administration
409 Third Street SW
Washington, DC 20416
(800) 205-6743
Get booklets and a possible loan
guarantee plus other help

Service Corps of Retired Executives
(Hotline) (800) 827-5722
Branches in most major cities offer
free advice and guidance.

Taxpayer Service Division
Internal Revenue Service
1111 Constitutional Ave NW
Washington DC 20224
(202) 622-5000
Can be very helpful to those
starting a small business

U.S. Department of Commerce
Washington, DC   20230
Ask for "Guides for Business" plus
other helpful booklets

U.S. Printing Office
Consumer Information Center
Pueblo, Colorado 81009
Ask for free catalog of booklets

These are just a few of the government agencies offering assistance and guidance . Also contact your local Chamber of Commerce and the Dept. of Commerce at your State's capitol. With a computer you can reach most agencies by email.

INDEPENDENT CONTRACTOR
AGREEMENT

This is to acknowledge that I. _____

_____ residing at _____

___in_____ have agreed to

work as an Independent Contractor of my services

to_____ of_____

_____

Under this arrangement I will not be an employee, will not be under direct supervision, will be free to determine the time I start and end my work and total number of hours, will not be covered by or participating in any insurance or employee benefits related to this work, will supply own tools, not have any deductions taken from my earnings for Social Security payments, unemployment compensation or federal income taxes.

This Independent Contractor arrangement can be terminated by either Party hereto by agreed 24-hour, courtesy notice to the other.

Agreement entered into this _____day of _____ 2004 .

Signed   _____
                    Independent Contractor

Note: A record must be kept of money paid to an Independent Contractor. If $600 or more, by January 31st Form 1099 must be supplied to Independent Contractor and to the IRS citing amount paid. Note: This form is offered as a guide, not as completely legal document for all Independent Contractor relationships.

RECOMMENDED BOOKS

One or more of the following books may be of value to you when launching a business. We take orders for them at $16.95 (books marked "A") or $12.95 (books marked "B"). The prices are guaranteed to be below the publisher's list price, but some may be dollar or two higher than a discounted price at a store. On some books we will make a few dollars, will lose a few dollars on others. Hopefully it will balance out in the end. *Important! - books are NOT returnable.*

With order please enclose a check or money-order in pre-payment (no cash), *adding $2 for postage and handling plus $1.50 for each additional book ordered.* The book(s) you choose will be sent to you within a few days. Books are a small investment to help you make a success of your business, can prevent costly mistakes.

Start And Run a Tour Guide Business (A)

How To Run A Catering Business From Home (A)

How To Start A House-Cleaning Business (B)

Selling Your Gourmet Food Specialty (From Home) (B)

Construction Clean-Up Business (A)

Start Your Own Temporary Help Business (A)

How To Start A Mail Order Business   (A)

Woodworker's Marketing Guide   (A)

How To Start A Coffee Bar (B)

Haynes Automobile Detailing Manual (B)

Massage: A Career At Your Fingertips (A)

What Prosperous Massage Therapists Know (B)

The Complete Book of Astrology (B)

How to Start A Home-Based Pet-Business (B)

How To Start a Day-Care Business From Home   B

How To Make Money Sewing At Home   (B)

What Color Is Your Pool (A Maintenance Guide) B)

Stage Producer's Guide   (B)

Your Successful Real Estate Career   (B)

Start Your Own Seminar Business (B)

Painting Contractor Business (B)

*Careers For Foreign Language/Multilingual Types
(B)*

Send check or money-order (no cash) with title(s) to

Taylor, Thomas & Lord - Book Sellers

762 South U.S. One Vero Beach, FL 32962

(Reminder: "A" books are $16.95, "B" books $12.95

Add $2 S & H, $1.50 per additional book) Thanks

A CLOSING WORD

Now that you have read through this book let me give you some unasked for advice. If you found one or more businesses that appeal to you, don't take impulsive steps, such as quitting your job or selling off the business you now may have, or going out and buying a truck or other expensive equipment, or leasing a place of business.

Enthusiasm is a necessary part of being successful at whatever one undertakes. It is not my purpose to dampen any enthusiasm you may have about a business. I just want to suggest that before you take any definitive actions -- like quitting your job --you think about the business for a few days. In the meantime discuss the business with your friends (not those where you work, they are wage slaves). Your spouse is not the right person for that discussion. A wife is security-oriented and usually hates the idea of taking chances, while a husband wants to be the main object of his wife's attention. The right time for a discussion with your spouse is just before you make the final decision-- on your own!

There are hundreds of businesses one can go into with very little capital. With a little imagination and serious thinking you probably can come up with some good ideas of your own? That thinking process will be helped by asking yourself a few questions: "What am I really good at?" "What would I really enjoy doing to make money?" "Can I make enough money doing that, so I (or my family) won't have to downgrade a present lifestyle?" "How much money will it take to get into that business?" "Is there presently so much competition in that business a newcomer will find it rough going?" Will I be taking a serious risk that will affect others I care about?"

Well, these are the kinds of questions to ask yourself. In short, go slow and go smart (that means " getting information"). Whatever you decide I sincerely wish you great success. When you are successful let me know, so you can inspire others.

Robb Roy Taylor

WILL THIS BOOK HELP YOU TO MAKE MORE MONEY?

In this book Robb Roy Taylor, a Business Opportunity Specialist for more than thirty years, describes SEVENTY businesses any man or woman can launch for a few hundred dollars--at most! Some require less than $100 to start, yet each can produce a good income when properly managed. Many of the businesses are unique and creative, usually will have no competitors .

Not only are details of the 70 businesses given, but also ideas for making the businesses successful. For example, low cost ways of promoting sales are described, and warnings given about mistakes many people make when starting and running a business.

Almost all of the 70 businesses described in this book can be run from home on a part-time basis. However, if you are not presently employed and need to earn money to pay bills. some of the 70 businesses can pay off quickly if run on a full-time basis. Most do NOT require special skills or abilities.

Some advantages and disadvantages of owning your own business are realistically set forth, including tax benefits, while several, so-called "Opportunities" are exposed as businesses to avoid.

70 Businesses   **$14.95**